The
Story of Jesus

The Story of JESUS

told by
Edmund Filmer

with pictures by
A. W. Lacey and S. W. Donnison

Lakeland

LAKELAND
116 BAKER STREET
LONDON W1M 2BB

First published 1954
This edition 1973

ISBN 0 551 00468 1

Printed in Spain by Editorial Fher S.A. Bilbao

To Parents

This is not a book of disconnected Bible stories, but a consecutive narrative in which the main events in the earthly life of Jesus are recorded in their true historical order. As the relationship between the various incidents becomes clear, and the story develops towards its dramatic climax in the trial, crucifixion and resurrection of Our Lord, children will be increasingly led to think about the meaning of these events, and finally to ask why did Jesus die: if He was truly God manifest in the flesh, why did he not save Himself? This question is far too frequently left unanswered. On pages 124, 127-9 and 130-1 the opportunity has been taken to provide an answer in a simple conversational form which is not thus recorded in the Gospels. This cannot be regarded as a departure from historical truth, for the Bible clearly states that these conversations did take place; we read, for example, in Luke 24. 45-46, " Then opened he their understanding that they might understand the Scriptures, and said unto them, Thus it behoved Christ to suffer." A conversation based on the most likely passages of Scripture has, therefore, been constructed, and Bible references will be found in the index on page 134.

Care has been taken to make the pictures agree as far as possible with all that is known about Palestine in the time of Our Lord. Apart from the figure of Jesus who, according to custom, is depicted as wearing a "toga", the style of clothing is the same as that which has always been worn in the land since Bible times; the artists wish to join in acknowledging their gratitude to the Rev. and Mrs. L. T. Pearson for their kindness in lending the dresses from which the pictures were painted. Those who look for details will find that each of the disciples is recognisable by his dress whenever he appears, except that those who were fishermen wear different clothes in Jerusalem from those they wear in Galilee.

Contents

CONTENTS

BACK IN JERUSALEM

JEALOUS JEWS

THE FINAL CONTEST

THE TRIAL

THE LAST SACRIFICE

RESURRECTION

BIBLE REFERENCES

Pictures

Maps

THE KING IS BORN

The Good News

MARY was really a princess of the tribe of Judah, but times were hard, so she lived in the country at Nazareth. Her people had been conquered by the Romans, who had made Herod, one of the hated Edomites, their king. He collected heavy taxes from them, partly for himself and partly to pay to his Roman overlords.

Mary was one of the few who still had faith in God, believing that soon he would send the promised Saviour to deliver her people from foreign rule. Like others who had read the Scriptures, she knew that the time was near.

One day God sent to her an angel named Gabriel. " Greetings, Mary! " he said. " You have been specially favoured by the Lord God and blessed among women."

At first Mary was frightened when she saw the angel, and wondered what this strange greeting might mean.

" Don't be frightened, Mary," the angel went on. " You have found favour with God. You are going to have a baby son, and you are to call him Jesus. He shall be great and be called the Son of the Most High. The Lord God will give to him the throne of his fore-father David, and he shall reign over the House of Jacob for ever; his kingdom shall have no end."

" How can that be," asked Mary, " seeing that I am not yet married? "

" The Holy Spirit will come upon you," replied Gabriel, " and for that reason your child shall be called the Son of God."

Now Mary was engaged to be married to Joseph, the carpenter. When he heard what the angel had said, he wondered whether he ought to marry her, but one night in a dream an angel appeared to him too.

" Joseph, son of David," he said, for Joseph, like Mary, was descended from King David, " don't be afraid to take Mary to be your wife, for her child is the Son of God. When he is born you are to call him Jesus, which means Jehovah the Saviour, for he shall save his people from their sins."

All this happened just as Isaiah the prophet had said long ago: " A virgin shall give birth to a son, and his name shall be Immanuel, which means God with us."

It was soon after this that Caesar Augustus, the Roman Emperor, made an order saying that all his subjects must be taxed. Everybody had to go to be registered in his native town. Joseph and Mary, who belonged to the family of David, had to go south to Bethlehem, for that was where David had lived. When they arrived, however, there were so many other people going for the same purpose that there was no more room in the inn, and they had to stay the night in a stable. It was there at Bethlehem that Jesus, the Son of God and coming king of Israel, was born. Because they had no cradle for him, they wrapped him up and laid him in a manger.

That night in the fields close by there were some shepherds keeping watch over their flocks. Suddenly an angel appeared to them, and the glory of the Lord shone round them so that they were all terrified.

" Don't be afraid," said the angel. " I bring you good news of great joy to all people. For your Saviour who is the Christ is born this day in David's city. This is the sign whereby you may know him: you will find the baby wrapped up and lying in a manger."

Then there appeared a mighty host of angels praising God and singing " Glory be to God in the highest, and on earth peace to all men who please him."

Then, as suddenly as they had come, the angels disappeared.

" Let's go into Bethlehem," said the shepherds, " and see what this is that the Lord has shown us."

So they hurried off and found Mary and Joseph with the baby lying in the manger. They told them and everyone else in the town how the angels had said that Jesus was their Saviour, the Christ whom God had promised.

Good news of great joy

Escape from Murder

WHEN Jesus was born in Bethlehem, certain wise men came to Jerusalem from the east. " Where is the new-born king of the Jews? " they asked. " We have seen his star rise in the east, and have come to bring him presents and to worship him."

The news that a new king of Israel had been born came to the ears of Herod, and he was angry, because he was a very jealous ruler. Already he had had his wife and some of his own children killed, because he was suspicious that they were plotting against him to take his throne. Calling together all the chief priests and the scribes who kept the books of the prophets, he asked them where the Christ, who was to be king of Israel, should be born.

" In Bethlehem," they said; " for it is written in the book of the prophet Micah: ' Thou Bethlehem, in the land of Judah, art not the least among the princes of Judah, for out of thee shall come a prince who shall rule over my people Israel.' "

Although Herod believed this prophecy to be true, he thought he was so clever that he could defeat God's plan and murder the baby Jesus! Secretly he called for the wise men from the east and asked them when the star had appeared, so that he might find out how old the baby was.

Then he told them, " You will find the child in Bethlehem; " but he added craftily, " when you have found him, bring me word where he is, so that I can go and worship him too." This was his plot to discover where the baby was and send someone there to kill him.

The wise men set off, and, guided by the star they had seen, soon found the baby Jesus with his mother Mary. They worshipped him and gave him presents, but they did not go back to tell Herod where he was, because in a dream God told them not to. They returned to their own country by another way.

When Herod found out that the wise men had gone away without coming to tell him where the child was, he was very angry. However, he knew that Jesus was only a baby, so he gave orders that all baby boys under two years of age in Bethlehem should be killed.

Meantime the angel of the Lord appeared to Joseph in a dream and warned him. " Take the young child and his mother," he said, " and escape into Egypt. Stay there until I give you word, for Herod is looking for the child and wants to kill him."

So Joseph took Mary and the baby Jesus and they escaped secretly by night into Egypt, while Herod's servants murdered all the baby boys in Bethlehem and the surrounding district.

It was shortly after this that Herod the Great died, and his kingdom was divided among his three sons: Archelaus ruled over Judaea and Samaria in the south; Herod Antipas governed the northerly provinces of Galilee and Peraea; while Philip ruled the country beyond Jordan to the north and east of the Sea of Galilee.

The angel of the Lord, therefore, appeared to Joseph again and said, " Arise, take the baby and his mother and return to the land of Israel, for those who wanted to kill the child are dead." So Joseph took the child and his mother and returned to the land of Israel.

Now when Joseph heard that Archelaus ruled over Judaea, and that he was even more cruel and wicked than his father, Herod the Great, he was afraid to go back. But God gave him instructions in a dream, and he went by another way through the province of Peraea back to Nazareth in the north. There he settled down and returned to his trade as a carpenter; while Mary brought up the young child Jesus.

Lost in Jerusalem

HEROD'S son Archelaus, who ruled over Judaea, was so cruel that it was not long before the Jews sent to Caesar Augustus in Rome to complain about him. When the Emperor heard what a bad ruler he was, he took him away and sent a Roman governor to rule over Judaea in his place. Only after that was it safe for Joseph and Mary to go up to Jerusalem each year to the Festival of the Passover.

As soon as Jesus was twelve years old, he, too, went up to Jerusalem with his parents at the time of the Passover. When he came to the great white temple, he was surprised to find that its outer court was more like a market square than a place of worship. The noise was terrible: above the bleating of sheep and the bellowing of cattle, there rose the voices of merchants and money-changers arguing and bargaining over their business.

Joseph and Mary had brought with them a lamb to sacrifice for the Passover. They had been very careful to see that it was spotless and perfect in every way, for the priests were very particular. It was said that they often found fault with lambs just to make people go and pay a high price for another from one of the traders in the temple court with whom they shared the profit.

When the lamb had been slain in the temple, they took it away and, after roasting it, ate it that night. This was a special feast in memory of the night when all the first-born children of Egypt were killed, and Moses led the people of Israel out of captivity. Jesus was the youngest at the feast, so it was his duty to ask, " What do you mean by this sacrifice? "

To this the oldest one present, who was Joseph, had to reply, " This is the Passover of the Lord which we eat, because the Lord passed over the houses of our fathers in Egypt." There were more questions and answers, and then they sang a song called " When Israel came out of Egypt."

When the time came for them to go home to Nazareth, Joseph and

He was talking with the doctors

Mary set out with their friends, but Jesus went back to the temple to listen to the teaching of the scribes. He had learnt the Scriptures so well at home that it was not long before he was talking with the doctors of the law, and asking them such thoughtful questions that they were amazed at his knowledge and understanding.

Meanwhile on the road to Nazareth Joseph and Mary had missed their boy, and came back to look for him. " Son," they said when they found him at last, " why have you behaved like this? Don't you know that we have been terribly worried looking for you? "

" Why should you be worried looking for me? " replied Jesus. " Surely you ought to have known that I should be in my Father's house! "

Although they did not understand what he meant by this, they never forgot what he had said. Meanwhile Jesus obediently went home with them to Nazareth, but he did not forget about the noisy traders in the temple court. He made up his mind that one day, when he was grown up, he would go and clean up all that wretched business.

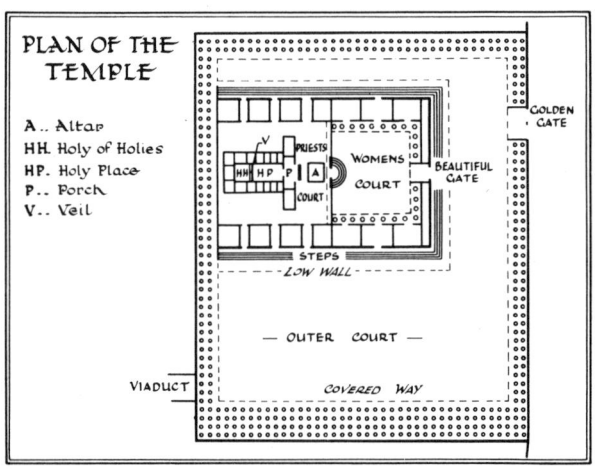

HIS TASK BEGINS

Preparing the Way

WHEN Jesus was about thirty years old, his cousin John the Baptist began to preach in the Judaean country along the river Jordan. He came to fulfil the prophecy given by Malachi many years before: " I shall send before me my messenger who shall prepare a way for me; and the Lord whom you seek shall suddenly come to his temple." Isaiah had also spoken of John, calling him " The voice of one crying in the desert, Prepare the way of the Lord and make his paths straight."

So it was that John told the people to change their wicked ways and give up their selfish habits, for the Lord himself was coming. " Repent," he said, " for the kingdom of heaven is at hand." Then he told them that they must be baptized in the Jordan as an outward sign that they were turning away from their sins.

From Jerusalem and all Judaea people crowded to hear him preach, and many were baptized. Some of the rich Pharisees from Jerusalem came as well, but John knew what rogues and swindlers many of them were.

" You brood of vipers! " he called them. " Who warned you to flee from the anger of God? Don't imagine you will escape by saying ' We are the children of Abraham.' You will have to show by your behaviour that you have become entirely different people."

" What must we do, then? " they asked.

Now John knew full well how the Pharisees got rich by cheating the poor, so he replied, " If you have two suits of clothes, give one to whoever has none; and if you have plenty to eat, share it with those who are hungry."

There were tax-collectors also who came to John, and they, too, asked him, " Master, what shall we do? "

" Don't charge people with more taxes than they ought to pay," he replied, knowing how they did this to make extra money.

There were some soldiers also, who asked, " What ought we to do? " and to them John said, " Don't frighten people or accuse them of crimes they have not committed. Be content with your pay, and don't ask for bribes in addition."

Now at that time there were many people who had read in the prophet Daniel that " from the time of the command to restore and to build Jerusalem until Christ the Prince shall be seven weeks and sixty-two weeks." They had worked out what this might mean, and as a result were expecting the Christ to come. They thought that perhaps John was the promised Prince, so they came to him and asked whether he were the Christ or not.

" I am baptizing you with water," replied John. " But there is one coming who is mightier than I, whose shoelace I am not worthy to untie. He shall baptize you with the Holy Spirit. He will gather together his chosen ones into his kingdom, but those who will not follow him he will cast into the fire."

After John the Baptist had been preaching for a while, Jesus came down from his home in Galilee to be baptized in the Jordan. John knew at once that Jesus was greater than he, and asked, " Why do you come to me to be baptized? Surely it is I who need to be baptized by you! "

" Let it be so now," replied Jesus, " for it is only right that I should set an example and fulfil every religious duty."

So John was persuaded and baptized him. As Jesus went up out of the water the heavens were opened and John saw the Holy Spirit descending on him like a dove. There came also a voice from heaven saying, " This is my beloved Son, in whom I am well pleased."

From that time John the Baptist knew for certain that Jesus was the Christ, the Son of God.

The Holy Spririt descending like a dove

Wrong Ways

WITH the baptism of the Holy Spirit Jesus had received power from his heavenly Father. Now he needed to be alone to consider how to use this power to do good, and to create a kingdom where people would be kind to one another and live freely and happily together. So he went away alone into the wild mountain country of Judaea to settle these problems.

There is nothing which can lead a man astray more than power, and Jesus, although the Son of God, was also a man; in fact he often called himself the Son of Man. For forty days he was tempted by Satan, the devil, to use his power in the wrong way.

In all that time he ate nothing. Then, when he realised how hungry he was, Satan spoke to him. " If you are the Son of God," he said, " why not command these stones to be made into bread? "

Jesus certainly had the power to do this: later he made five small loaves and two fish into enough food for more than five thousand people. But he would not use this power to satisfy his own hunger. If he started, even in a very small way, to use powers that other men did not possess, simply to make his own life easier, there would be no end to such uses. How, then, could he set an example to others, if he had this unfair advantage over them? He had come into the world to live as a man, so he could not do anything for himself that a man could not do. He must wait until his heavenly Father gave him bread, just as God had given the Israelites food during their forty years in the desert.

In reply to Satan Jesus used God's own words, spoken on that very occasion: " It is written," he said, " that man shall not live on bread alone, but by every word that comes from the mouth of God."

Next the devil took Jesus up into a high mountain, and showed him in a moment of time all the kingdoms of the world and all their riches and glory. " All these things will I give you," said Satan, " if you will fall down and worship me."

Now Satan had been made prince of this world from the beginning, so he had it in his power to give away the kingdoms of this world. But Satan's rule is one of force, and many a time he has given this power to dictators who are willing to serve him. Although Jesus longed to rule over all the kingdoms of the earth, he would not do so as Satan's servant, for this would make him the greatest dictator of all. His kingdom was to be one in which everyone obeyed him because they loved him, and not because he forced them to.

Once more Jesus quoted Scripture in reply: " It is written," he said, " you must worship the Lord your God, and him alone shall you serve."

Again Satan came to tempt Jesus, and took him in a vision up to the highest tower of the temple. " If you are the Son of God," he said, " jump down from here, for it is written: ' He will give orders to his angels that they should look after you, lest at any time you strike your foot against a stone.' "

Now if Jesus were to do this, or perform any other startling miracle, it would be sure to convince a great many people that he was the Son of God. They would no doubt admire him and would be glad to make him king, but it would not help them to love him or love one another, and still less would it teach them how to live better lives.

In each of these temptations Satan was trying to get Jesus to act without God's authority and set up a kingdom in the wrong way. So Jesus answered him again in the words of Scripture: " It is written," he said, " you must not challenge the Lord your God."

After this third defeat the devil left Jesus and the angels came and cared for him.

Choosing his Men

WHILE Jesus was away in the mountains John continued to preach and baptize in the river Jordan. His teaching had caused such a sensation that the Jews in Jerusalem sent a party of priests and Levites to find out more about him.

" Who are you? " they asked. " Are you the Christ? "

" No! " he told them plainly. " I am not the Christ."

" Who are you, then? " they asked. " Are you Elijah, or the prophet whom Moses promised? "

" No! " replied John. " I am neither of them."

"Well, tell us who you are," they insisted, "so that we can take word to those who sent us. What have you got to say about yourself? "

" I am the one of whom the prophet Isaiah spoke," answered John—" the voice of one crying in the desert, Prepare the way of the Lord and make his paths straight."

Still they went on questioning him. " Why do you baptize people if you are not the Christ, nor Elijah, nor that prophet? "

" I only baptize with water," replied John. " But there is one already here whom you do not know: he will come after me, and is so much greater than I that I am not worthy to stoop down and untie his shoelace."

The next day Jesus returned from the mountains, and when John saw him coming he said, " Look! This is the Lamb of God who will take away the sin of the world. This is the one of whom I said that he is so much greater than I."

Then John told them what he had seen: " I saw the Holy Spirit coming down upon him like a dove from heaven. At first I did not know who he was; but he that sent me to baptize with water told me this, that when I should see the Holy Spirit come down and rest upon anyone, this would be the one who would baptize with the Holy Spirit. I saw this, and can give evidence that this is the Son of God."

On the following day John the Baptist was standing by the river Jordan with two of his followers, who were fishermen from Galilee.

He upset the tables

One of them was also called John, and the other was Andrew.

" Look! The Lamb of God! " said the Baptist, as Jesus came down to the river.

Immediately John and Andrew began to follow Jesus, but when he saw them behind him, he turned and asked them what they wanted.

" We want to see where you live," they replied simply.

" Well, come with me and I will show you," said Jesus.

So they went and stayed with him that day.

Now Andrew had a brother called Peter, and he went to fetch him. " We have found the Christ," he said excitedly. " Come with me and meet the Lord." So Peter joined the little band.

The next day Jesus was going to set out for home, but first he met a man from Bethsaida whose name was Philip. " Come along with us," invited Jesus.

Philip had a friend called Nathanael, and he went off to bring him as well. " We have found him about whom Moses and all the prophets wrote," said Philip. " He is Jesus of Nazareth."

" I never read in the prophets that any good thing should come out of Nazareth," replied Nathanael doubtfully.

" Well, come and see for yourself," said Philip, who was not going to argue about it.

" Here comes a good honest Israelite," exclaimed Jesus when he saw Nathanael.

" How do you know anything about me? " asked Nathanael.

" Before Philip called you," replied Jesus, " I saw you under that fig-tree."

Now Nathanael had been quite alone praying to God under the fig-tree, so he knew who Jesus must be. " You are the Son of God! " he exclaimed, " You are surely the king of Israel! "

" So you believe in me because I said I saw you under the fig-tree," said Jesus. " You will see greater wonders than that."

Jesus had now chosen his first followers, and they all went back to Galilee, where Jesus made his home at Capernaum, a town on the shore of the lake.

VISITS TO THE CAPITAL

Driving out the Robbers

WHEN the time of the Passover came, Jesus went south again to Jerusalem. In the great courtyard of the temple he found the same evil trade being carried on just as it had been when he was a boy. There were the merchants selling oxen, sheep and doves at high prices to poor people who needed them for sacrifices; there were the money-changers who cheated everyone.

This could not be allowed to go on. Knotting together some short pieces of rope to make a whip, Jesus drove the merchants out of the temple along with their sheep and oxen. He upset the tables of the money-changers, and scattered their coins on the ground.

" Take these things away," he cried to those who sold doves, " and don't turn my Father's house into a market-place."

The leaders of the Jews were afraid to stop him, because he spoke so boldly as one having authority. When they heard him call the temple his Father's house, they asked, " What sign can you give us to show that you have a right to do these things? "

" If you destroy this temple," Jesus replied, " I will raise it up again in three days."

The Jews had no intention of destroying their fine new temple just to see whether Jesus could build it again in three days. " This temple has taken forty-six years to build," they said. " How, then, can you raise it up in three days? "

Jesus made no reply, for he had spoken of his own body as a temple, meaning that if they killed him he would rise from the dead within three days.

That night there was great excitement in the city. Everywhere people were talking about the young teacher who had dared to challenge the Jewish rulers and condemn their evil trading. The Pharisees were furious at this attack, but one of them, named Nicodemus, admired Jesus for what he had done. No doubt he had

heard from John the Baptist that the kingdom of heaven was at hand, and hoped that Jesus would put an end to the evil in the temple and set up an honest government.

Secretly, so that none of the other Pharisees would know, he came to Jesus by night.

" Master," he began, " we know that you are a teacher who has come from God."

Jesus understood at once that this man wanted to know about the kingdom of God. He was always willing to help anyone who believed in him and wanted to know the truth.

" Let me first make this clear," said Jesus—" unless a man is born again he cannot see the kingdom of God."

" I can't understand that," said Nicodemus, looking puzzled. " How can a man be born again when he is old? "

" Unless a new spirit be born in a man," explained Jesus, " he cannot enter the kingdom of God. All who are born of earthly parents are earthly; but you must have a new spirit within you that is born of the Spirit of God: that is why I say you must be born again."

" Well, how can that come about? " asked Nicodemus.

" Perhaps if I tell you of earthly things," Jesus went on, " you may be able to understand when I tell you of heavenly things. You remember that when the Israelites were bitten by deadly snakes in the desert, Moses set up a brazen serpent on a pole, and everyone who looked at it was saved. In the same way mankind was poisoned by that old serpent Satan in the garden of Eden, and I, the Son of Man, must be lifted up on a cross so that everyone who trusts in me may be saved.

" For God so loved the world that he gave his only Son, so that whoever believes in him should have everlasting life. This is the truth, and everyone who believes it is saved. Wicked people do not care for the truth, so they do not believe it, and therefore they are condemned."

Nicodemus was willing to believe the truth, and so he proved that night that even a Pharisee could be born again.

A woman came to draw water

The Woman at the Well

AFTER his visit to Jerusalem for the Passover Jesus stayed for a while to teach in the land of Judaea, but when the Pharisees heard that even more people came to hear him than went to listen to John the Baptist, they became jealous, so Jesus decided to go home to Galilee.

Usually the Jews would not go through the province of Samaria, because they disliked the Samaritans who were foreigners. That made no difference to Jesus—he wanted to go through Samaria.

One day, after a long walk in the hot sun, he and his friends came to a well which had been dug many years before by Jacob. Jesus was very tired, so he sat down by the well while his friends went into the town nearby to fetch something to eat. Presently a woman came to draw water from the well, so Jesus asked her to give him a drink.

" How is it, " she asked, " that you, being a Jew, ask a drink of me who am a woman of Samaria? " She was surprised because usually the Jews would never speak to the Samaritans.

" If you knew who it is who is asking you for a drink," replied Jesus, " and if you knew what God has to give, you would have asked me, and I would have given you living water."

" But, Sir," said the woman, looking puzzled, " you have nothing to draw with, and the well is deep. Where can you get that living water? Are you a greater man than Jacob who gave us this well and drank of it himself? "

" Whoever drinks from this well," explained Jesus, " becomes thirsty again; but the living water that I give does not come from a well such as this. It is like a fountain that springs up within you to give you everlasting life."

" Sir, please give me that water," said the woman, eager to learn more. " Then I shall not be thirsty and have to come here to draw water."

Now Jesus does not give the water of life to those who are not willing to give up their wicked ways, so he began to speak to the woman about her sins. She was shocked to find that he knew all about them, but like most people she didn't want to talk about such things.

"I see you are a prophet," she said, changing the subject. "Tell me now, who is right: our people say that we ought to worship God on that mountain yonder, but the Jews say that Jerusalem is the proper place."

"The Jews are quite right," said Jesus patiently; "God has chosen Jerusalem. But the time will soon come when people will worship God neither on this mountain nor in Jerusalem. God is spirit, and may be worshipped anywhere by those who truly seek him."

The woman had never heard anything like this before. "I know that the Christ is coming," she said. "I expect he will be able to explain all these things to us."

"I, who am speaking to you, am he," said Jesus.

Just then Jesus' friends came back from the town and were surprised to find him talking to a woman, but they were afraid to ask what she wanted. However, she was so excited to learn that Jesus was the Christ, that she left her water-pot and ran off to the town to tell her friends.

"Come and see a man who told me all that I ever did!" she cried. "Surely he must be the Christ!"

Quite a number of people were interested in what she said, so they came out to look for Jesus at the well. After they had seen and spoken to him, they asked him to come and stay with them for a while. So Jesus stayed there two days and told them more about the things of God, and many of them believed in him.

"Now we believe in him," they said to the woman, "not only on account of what you told us, but because we have heard him for ourselves, and know that he is indeed the Christ who has come to save the world."

So after two days Jesus left them and went on to his home in Galilee.

In Trouble for doing Good

THE NEXT time that Jesus went up to Jerusalem to one of the festivals, he passed by the pool of Bethesda. Near the pool were five arches, and in these lay a great many invalids who were lame or blind. From time to time the water used to bubble up, and it was said that whoever first entered the water after it was disturbed, would be cured of whatever sickness he had. All these invalids lay waiting for the water to bubble up.

Among them was a man who had been ill for thirty-eight years. The poor fellow had no friends to help him, and when the pool was disturbed he was so helpless that someone else always got into the water before him.

As Jesus passed by, this man looked up at him and their eyes met. At once Jesus knew that he had been helpless for a long time, and he felt sorry for him.

" Do you want to be made well? " he asked kindly.

" Yes, indeed I do, sir," replied the man. " But I have no one to help me into the pool when the water is disturbed; while I am trying to get there myself, someone else always gets in before me."

" Stand up! " said Jesus. " Take up your mat and walk."

Immediately the man found that he was completely cured, and was able to pick up his mat and walk home.

Now it happened to be the Sabbath day, and the Jews were very particular about what was allowed on the Sabbath. God's law, given them by Moses, had said that no work was to be done, but the Jews had added a lot of extra rules to say that all kinds of things were to be called work, and must not be done on the Sabbath.

When they saw this man carrying his mat they called out to him, " It is the Sabbath day; you are not allowed to carry your mat! "

After explaining how he had been marvellously cured, the invalid told them, " It was the one who cured me who told me to take up my mat and walk home."

" Who was it who told you to do that? " they asked him angrily,

33

Take up your mat and walk

for they did not seem to be in the least interested in the fact that he was healed. All they cared about was to make trouble for the man who had given such orders. " Who told you to carry your mat on the Sabbath day? " they demanded.

" I don't know who he was," the man replied: " he disappeared in the crowd."

Later Jesus found the man in the temple and said to him, " Listen; now that you are well again you must sin no more, or something worse will happen to you."

After this second meeting with Jesus the man went and told the Jews that it was Jesus who had cured him. The Jews, therefore, began to make trouble for Jesus, because he had cured a man on the Sabbath day, and then told him to carry his mat. Some of them even went so far as to talk of putting him to death.

When they came and accused him of this, he said, " My heavenly Father works all the time, and therefore so do I."

That only made the Jews even more eager to kill him, because he not only broke the Sabbath, but also said that God was his Father, thus making himself equal with God.

" Let me tell you this," Jesus added. " I can do nothing of myself—I can only do what I see my heavenly Father doing: whatever he does, I do the same."

The Jews, however, would not believe he was the Son of God. It was just as Jesus had said to Nicodemus: these people could not believe in him because they were wicked.

" You sent to enquire of John the Baptist," Jesus said, " and he gave you his evidence about me. But the evidence that I give you is even stronger. The works that my Father has given me to do are these good deeds that I am now doing, and they are the evidence that my Father has sent me."

But because their deeds were evil the Jews would not believe the truth.

TEACHING IN GALILEE

Promises Come True

WHEN Jesus returned to Galilee he went from one village to another teaching about the kingdom of God. The country folk listened to him gladly, and he was soon famous all over the district. When he came to Nazareth, where he had been brought up, he went to the synagogue on the Sabbath day, as was his custom, and stood up to read the lesson.

He was given the book of the prophet Isaiah, and when he had found the place he read: " The Spirit of the Lord is upon me, because he has appointed me to preach good news to the poor; to comfort the broken-hearted, to set the captives free, to give sight to the blind, relief to those under oppression and to proclaim the year of acceptance with the Lord." Then he closed the book and, returning it to the minister, began to preach, taking this passage as his text.

" Today," he began, " this scripture is fulfilled in your hearing." But as soon as he told them that he was already setting up the kingdom of God in which all this would happen, the people began to doubt.

" Surely," they said, " he is nothing more than a carpenter's son."

" I suppose," Jesus went on, " that you expect me to repeat here all the miracles that I have done in other places. But I tell you that a prophet is never welcomed in his own country. You remember that in the days of Elijah there was a famine for three and a half years; there were many widows in Israel in those days, but Elijah was sent to none of them, but only to a Syrian woman. There were also many lepers in Israel in the time of Elisha, but none of them was healed but Naaman, who was a Syrian."

When the people were reminded of these cases when Elijah and Elisha had been sent to foreigners, they were furious, and drove Jesus out of their synagogue. But when they tried to push him over a cliff, he passed quietly through the crowd and disappeared.

Friends at Home

FTER that, Jesus went home to Capernaum where the people were willing to listen to him. There he was able to show them, by his kindness in curing sick folk, how people should behave in his kingdom.

One day he met his old friend Simon Peter and Andrew, his brother, fishing on the shore of the lake.

" Come along with me," he called, " and I will make you fishers of men." Immediately they left their nets and followed him.

A little further on they found James and John with Zebedee, their father, mending their nets. Jesus called to them too, and they left their father with his servants and followed him.

On the Sabbath day they went into the synagogue and Jesus began to preach. All the people were astonished at his teaching, for it was clear that he knew what he was talking about.

In the synagogue was a man possessed by a demon, who called out, " I know who you are! You are the Holy One of God! "

" Be quiet," said Jesus, " and come out of him."

At first the demon threw the poor man into another fit, but soon left him in his right mind.

Everyone marvelled at this: " This is something quite new," they said. " He even gives orders to evil spirits and they obey him! " So the news of it spread through the whole district.

After the service Jesus went home with his disciples to get something to eat, but they were disappointed. They found that Simon Peter's mother-in-law, who was to have prepared the food, had suddenly been taken ill. Jesus, however, just took her by the hand, and she recovered immediately and was able to get them their meal.

When the Sabbath day ended at sunset, all the people in the town brought out those who were ill and those who were possessed by demons, and gathered in a great crowd outside the door of the house where Jesus lived. So he went out and laid his hands on them, and cured them all.

Catching Fish

THE NEXT morning the people came again and asked Jesus not to go away.

"But I must preach the good news of the kingdom of God in other towns as well," he told them; "for that is what I have been sent to do."

So Jesus went about all Galilee teaching in the synagogues and curing those who were sick, but later he came back to Capernaum.

One night Peter and Andrew, James and John went out fishing, but caught nothing. In the morning, while they were washing their nets, Jesus came along and began to teach the people on the shore. Soon there was such a crowd that he had to get into Peter's boat and push out a little way from the land. There he sat down and taught the people from the ship.

After he had finished he said to Peter, "Row out into deep water and let down the nets."

"But, Master," replied Peter doubtfully, "we have worked all night and caught nothing. But if you say so, we will try again.

This they did, and caught so many fish that their net broke.

"Hi! Come and give us a hand!" they called to James and John, who were still on the shore with the other boat.

They came out at once to help, and soon both ships were so full of fish that they almost sank.

Now Peter was an old hand at fishing, and he knew that in deep water the fish could easily escape below the net. When he saw all this quantity of fish drawn into the net, he was amazed that Jesus could work such a miracle.

"Lord," he said, "I am a sinful man, and not fit to be with you."

"Don't be afraid," replied Jesus. "From now on you shall come with me and fish for men. It may not look easy, but I will draw the people to me."

Up till then they had been helping Jesus only in their spare time, but now they became full-time disciples.

THE PHARISEES MAKE TROUBLE

The Trouble Starts

ONE DAY a leper came to Jesus and, kneeling before him, asked to be healed. In those days there was no cure for this terrible disease, which was so catching that those who suffered from it were turned out of the city until they died. If a leper met anyone, he had to walk on the other side of the road calling out, " Unclean! Unclean! "

This poor leper was very ill, yet he trusted in Jesus to save him. " Lord," he said, " if you are willing, I know that you can make me clean."

Jesus felt so sorry for him that he put out his hand and touched him. " I am willing," he said. " Be clean! " And immediately the man was restored to health.

" On no account," Jesus told him, " must you tell anyone about this; only go and show yourself to the priest, and take with you the gift which the law of Moses demands, in order that you may be declared clean."

No sooner had the man been to the priest, however, than he began to go round telling everyone that Jesus had touched him and made him well. The result was that Jesus became more famous than ever, and people flocked to hear him speak and to be cured of their diseases.

Now the scribes and Pharisees were not at all pleased to see everybody going to listen to Jesus rather than to them, for they thought that they were the only people who knew anything about religion and the laws of Moses. Because they were jealous of Jesus they tried to find fault with him.

There was a rule that anyone who touched a leper was unclean, so some of the Pharisees wanted to make out that Jesus was unclean because he had touched a leper. Others said that, because the man was no longer ill, it could not be proved that Jesus had touched a leper. This was just the kind of thing that the lawyers loved to argue over.

So it came about on a certain day, when Jesus was teaching in Capernaum, that there were Pharisees and doctors of the law sitting by who had come out of every town in Galilee, and even some from Judaea and Jerusalem. Besides them the house was packed to the doors with crowds of people who had come to hear about the kingdom of heaven and to be cured of their diseases.

One unhappy man, who was paralysed and wanted to be cured, had got four of his friends to carry him there in his bed. When they found that there was such a crowd that they could not get in, they climbed up to the roof. There they removed some of the tiling and let down the bed in which the sick man lay into the middle of the meeting below.

Jesus knew that this man's disease had been brought on through his own sin, but that now he was really sorry for what he had done. So he said to him, " Cheer up, son, your sins are forgiven."

When they heard this, some of the scribes who were sitting by said to one another, " What's this? Surely this is blasphemy! No one has the power to forgive sins but God alone."

Jesus knew at once what they were saying. " With what evil purpose do you start these arguments? " he asked them. " It is just as easy for me to say, Your sins are forgiven, as to say, Get up and walk." Then he challenged them to admit that he was God by adding, " But to prove to you that I have the power to forgive sin, I say to this man whose illness was caused by sin, Arise, take up your bed, and go home."

Immediately the man got up in front of the whole crowd of them, picked up the rug on which he lay, and walked out praising God.

The effect on the crowd was tremendous. The scribes and Pharisees were amazed, while the rest of the people gave glory to God, saying, " We have certainly seen strange things today. We never saw anything like this before."

40

They let down the bed

The Tax-Collector

MANY a time Jesus passed by the little customs office where Matthew sat collecting the taxes from merchants bringing their wares into Capernaum from beyond Jordan, or from boatmen landing fish from the lake. All who brought goods across the border into Galilee had to pay customs duty.

Matthew was a secret admirer of Jesus and often listened to him teaching, but it would have been most improper for him to speak to him, for, as a tax-collector, he was an outcast, almost as bad as a leper. Nobody likes paying taxes, and the Jews particularly hated those who helped their Roman overlords to take away their money.

Jesus had noticed Matthew too. He saw that he was a man who would not overcharge people in order to put extra money in his own pocket, like most of the tax-collectors did. One day, as he passed by, he called out to him, " Matthew! Come and be one of my disciples."

Matthew was delighted, and left his job at the customs office right away. But he did not desert his old friends. First he invited Jesus and his disciples to a grand party at his house. Then he asked his fellow tax-collectors, and other people he knew who had fallen into evil ways, to come and meet this new master of his, who could show them how to make a fresh start and lead better lives.

When the scribes and Pharisees saw Jesus and his disciples going to a party with tax-collectors, they thought it was disgraceful, and said to them, " Why do you sit down to eat and drink at the same table with all these horrible tax-collectors and sinners? "

When Jesus heard this he replied, " Those who are healthy require no doctor, but only those who are ill. In the same way I have not come to help the righteous, but those who have gone wrong and want to lead better lives."

Fault-Finding

IT WAS not long before the Pharisees thought of something else to complain about. It was their custom to fast twice a week as well as on the Sabbath day, and they thought that every respectable Jew should do the same. Although no such fast days were mentioned in the law of Moses, the rule was so strict that even John the Baptist and his followers kept it.

So the Pharisees came to Jesus and asked, " Why do your disciples go to parties, when all respectable people are fasting and saying their prayers? "

" Among my friends," Jesus answered, " I am like the bridegroom at a wedding, so how can you expect them to fast while I am with them? But the time will come when I shall be taken away; then they will fast.

" You don't fix a new patch on an old garment, for it would only tear it and make it worse. Nor do you put new wine in old wine-skins, for they won't stretch and would soon burst. In the same way my new teaching cannot be made to fit in with your old hard-and-fast rules."

On the following Sabbath day, as Jesus was walking through the fields, his disciples were hungry, so they began to pick ears of corn, rubbing them in their hands and eating the grain. When the Pharisees saw them doing this, they again took the opportunity to find fault with Jesus. They made out that picking corn was reaping, and rubbing the ears was threshing, both of which counted as work, and must not be done on the Sabbath.

So they asked Jesus, " Why do your disciples do that which is not lawful on the Sabbath day? "

Patiently Jesus answered them. " Have you not even read enough to know what David did when he was hungry? He went into the house of God and took some of the shewbread for himself and his friends, even though it was not lawful for anyone except the priests to eat it."

" I would have you know this," he added. " The Sabbath was made for the good of man, not man for keeping the Sabbath. If you had only taken notice that God has said, ' I prefer mercy and not sacrifices,' you would never make such foolish accusations."

The scribes and Pharisees saw that they were getting nowhere by merely making complaints. What they needed was to prove Jesus wrong in front of all the people. If they could only show that he was a law-breaker, they hoped that the people would give up following him. On the next Sabbath day, therefore, they brought a man with a withered hand into the synagogue, and waited to see whether Jesus would cure him. If he did so, they meant to accuse him before the whole congregation of breaking the Sabbath law.

Jesus, however, knew their thoughts, and when he stood up in the synagogue he said kindly to the man with the withered hand, " Come and stand out here in front."

The man got up and stood out in front of everyone.

" Now," said Jesus, addressing the people, " Which of you would refuse to pull a sheep out of a pit, if it had fallen into it on the Sabbath day? Surely a man is better than a sheep! So I will ask you one thing; is it lawful to do good on Sabbath days, or to do evil; to save life, or to kill? "

The Pharisees had no answer to this, and remained silent as Jesus looked round at them with anger, though grieved that they remained so obstinate.

" Stretch out your hand! " he said at last to the man who stood in front of him.

He stretched out his hand, and immediately it became as strong as the other.

The Pharisees were furious. As soon as they had left the synagogue, they got together to talk over what they could do about Jesus, and even went to Herod's friends to get their help in putting Jesus to death.

44

THE KINGDOM EXPLAINED

Lessons on the Hillside

THE PHARISEES were making life more and more difficult for Jesus in Capernaum, but when he heard that they were plotting to get rid of him he decided it was time to go away. Once already the Jews in the synagogue at Nazareth had tried to murder him, and he had no desire to get mixed up in any further violence, for he still had much to do. So, as it was summer, he went off in a boat on the lake with his disciples and landed away out in the country.

A great many of the country folk followed him there, some of them coming from distant parts to be cured of their diseases. These he strictly told that they should not let it be known where he was, for he did not want the Pharisees to come and start any more arguments. Isaiah, the prophet, had foretold of him: " See my servant whom I have chosen, my beloved in whom I am well pleased: he shall not argue nor shout, neither shall he raise his voice in the streets."

One evening he went up into the mountains and spent the night praying to his heavenly Father for guidance, for he had important work to do. In the morning he called his disciples together and chose twelve of them to be called apostles. These were the fishermen Simon Peter and his brother Andrew, and their partners James and John, the sons of Zebedee. With Philip and Nathanael they had been his followers since the day when they left John the Baptist by the Jordan. Then there was Matthew, the tax-collector, and five new disciples: first Thomas, then James the son of Alphaeus, Jude his brother, Simon Zelotes, and Judas Iscariot. All these Jesus chose to help him in preaching, in curing the sick and in driving out evil spirits.

Then he sat down on the hillside and began to teach them about the kingdom of God and the kind of people he was going to have in it.

" Blessed are those of you who are poor now," he began, " for yours is the kingdom of God. But woe betide the rich, for they have had their reward already.

" Blessed are those who long for justice and fair play, for their desires shall be satisfied. Blessed are those who stand up for what is right, even if they are ill-treated and have to suffer for it; they are the people who will come into the kingdom of God. If people laugh at you and tell all kinds of wicked lies about you for my sake, then you should really be very glad, for great shall be your reward in my kingdom. But take care when everyone praises you and says what a fine fellow you are, for that is what they said to the false prophets in the old days.

" You are the light of the world. Just as no one puts a lamp under a basket, but sets it up on a lamp-stand where it can be seen, so should you let your own good behaviour be seen by all, so that they may praise God on your account."

While Jesus was telling his disciples all this, more and more people were gathering round to hear his teaching about the kingdom of God.

" Don't imagine," Jesus went on, " that I have come to do away with the law; on the contrary, I have come to help you to fulfil it. For I tell you that unless you behave a great deal better than the scribes and Pharisees, you have no hope of entering the kingdom of heaven.

" You have heard them say that you should love your neighbour and hate your enemy: but I tell you to love your enemies and do good to those that hate you. For your heavenly Father makes the sun shine on bad people as well as on good. So bless them that curse you and pray for those that ill-treat you. If you do good only to those that love you, you are no better than the wicked, for they do that much too, so what reward can you expect? "

Many other things Jesus told them about his kingdom, and all the people were amazed at his teaching, for he had spoken as one having authority, and not like the scribes.

Help for a Roman

WHEN Jesus had finished teaching his disciples, they all returned to Capernaum before setting out on their first missionary tour of Galilee. As they approached the town, some of them wondered whether they might not be in danger from their enemies who were lying in wait for them. Almost at once a party of rulers from the synagogue approached them.

" Lord," they said, " the commander of the garrison has sent us to ask you to come and cure his servant of whom he is very fond. He is lying paralysed and in great pain, almost at the point of death." Then, thinking that Jesus would not help a foreigner, they added, " He certainly deserves this favour, for he loves our nation and built us our synagogue."

" I will come and help him," said Jesus without hesitation, and set off through the town.

They had almost reached the house, when the commander sent another messenger, saying, " I am not fit for you to come under my roof, nor did I think myself fit to come and see you myself. Just speak the word, and my servant will be well. For I, too, am a man with authority, having others under me: I say to one, Go, and he goes; to another, Come, and he comes; and to my servant, Do this, and he does it."

When Jesus heard this he was amazed. " Listen to that," he said to the crowd. " I never saw such great faith; no, not even in Israel. And I can tell you," he added, " that many shall come from east and west and sit down with Abraham, Isaac and Jacob in the kingdom of heaven, but many of you will be thrown into outer darkness."

Then, turning to those who had come to him for help, he said, " Go and tell your master that just as he has believed so has it been done."

And they went home and found that the servant had got well at that very moment.

God save the son of David !

Help for a Jew

THE CURING of the Roman commander's servant provided the disciples with a fine example of how to put into practice their Master's lesson on loving their enemies. However, they had no time to notice its effect on the scribes and Pharisees, for early next morning Jesus took them out on their first missionary journey. He was eager to start training them to preach and heal the sick.

During the summer months they went about through all the towns and villages of Galilee telling the people the good news about the kingdom of God. Then they crossed over to the eastern shores of the Sea of Galilee to the country of Decapolis. There Jesus restored a lunatic to his right mind, for he had been possessed by so many demons that he was called Legion. From there they took a boat back across the lake, and at last came home to Capernaum, where crowds of people were waiting on the shore to welcome Jesus, for they had all been looking forward to seeing him again.

Now Jairus, the chief of the council of the synagogue in Capernaum, had an only daughter about twelve years of age. She had been taken very ill and no one had been able to cure her. So, as soon as Jesus landed in Capernaum, Jairus came and knelt at Jesus' feet, worshipping him and imploring him to come and help him.

" My little daughter," he said, " is lying at the point of death. Please come and lay your hands on her so that she may get better and live."

Here was another opportunity for Jesus to do good, so he went along with Jairus at once, while the crowd followed them through the narrow streets.

Among the crowd was a woman who had been troubled with a serious disease for twelve years. Already she had spent all her money on going to doctors, but none of them had done her any good; in fact she had become rather worse. When she heard how Jesus could cure people by just touching them, she came up behind him in the crowd and touched the hem of his clothes, saying to herself, " If only I touch his clothes I shall be cured." And so it was, for immediately she felt herself to be quite well.

Jesus knew at once that power had gone out from him, so he turned and asked, " Who touched my clothes? "

His disciples, not having noticed the woman, were surprised. " What do you mean " they asked, " by ' who touched you?' when there are all these people crowding round you? "

When the woman saw that Jesus was looking for her, she came forward, trembling with fear, and knelt before him. She told him all about her trouble, and why she had touched his clothes.

" Daughter," said Jesus, " don't worry! Your faith has made you well."

While Jesus had been speaking to this woman, a messenger came to Jairus from his home. " Your daughter is dead," he said. " There is no need to trouble the Master any further."

When Jesus heard this he went on his way to the house, saying to Jairus, " Don't worry! Only believe, and she will recover."

Arriving at the house, he went in, taking Peter, James and John. There was a great commotion, people wailing and weeping aloud.

" Make way! " said Jesus, as he walked in. " Why make all this fuss? The girl isn't dead; she's only asleep."

All the people laughed at this, for they were sure she was dead. So Jesus put them all outside and took only the father and mother and the three disciples into the room where the girl lay. There he took the child by the hand and said, " Little girl, wake up! "

Immediately the girl got up from her bed, to the wonder and astonishment of her parents.

" And now you must give her something to eat," said Jesus to her mother, " for I'm sure she must be hungry."

As he left them he said, " Don't tell anyone else about this," but they could not restrain themselves, and it was not long before the story had spread all over the country.

HEAVENLY FOOD

Feeding the Five Thousand

JESUS had shown such kindness to the Roman commander whose servant was cured, and to Jairus whose little girl had been raised from her death-bed, that nobody in Capernaum wanted to harm him any more. So he was able to go on teaching and healing the sick without being troubled by his enemies.

Calling together his twelve disciples, he gave them power to drive out demons and cure the sick, and then sent them out by two and two.

During the winter months the disciples travelled around preaching and healing: but their work was not without danger, for Herod put John the Baptist in prison and later beheaded him. In the spring they came home to tell Jesus all that had happened, and a great many people from all over the country followed them, bringing with them those that needed help.

" I think we should all go away for a holiday," said Jesus. " There are so many people coming here that we scarcely have time to eat! "

So they set off secretly in their boat for Bethsaida, and from there walked up into the hills beyond Jordan. Some of the people saw them going, however, so it was not long before the crowds followed them on foot along the shore. Soon there was a vast multitude with them there, and because they seemed so lost and helpless, like sheep without a shepherd, Jesus began to teach them again, and heal those that were sick.

Evening was coming on, when the disciples came to Jesus and said, " This is a very desolate spot and the time is getting late; don't you think we had better send the people away so that they can go into the villages to buy themselves food? "

" There is no need for that," replied Jesus. " You can give them a meal."

" Do you want us to go and buy bread for them all? " they asked. looking surprised.

Little girl, wake up !

Jesus turned to Philip, who was a native of Bethsaida and would know that so much food could not be found in those parts. " Where can we get enough bread for all these people? " he asked. Jesus had already made up his mind what he would do, but he wanted to test Philip.

" It would cost a lot of money," replied Philip, " even if each person had only a little."

" Go and see how many loaves you have," said Jesus to the other disciples.

At that moment Andrew came forward leading a small boy. " There's a lad here," he said, " who has five barley rolls and a couple of small fish. But what are they among so many? " There were about five thousand men there besides the women and children.

" Tell all the people to sit down on the grass in parties of fifty," said Jesus.

When they had done this, he took the five barley rolls and two fish from the boy and, looking up to heaven, he gave thanks and broke the bread and divided the fishes, giving them to the disciples to take to the people. As long as he went on dividing up the food and giving it to the disciples, there was a supply until all the people were satisfied.

Then Jesus told his disciples to go and collect any food which remained over so that nothing should be wasted. Each of the twelve returned with a basket full of food.

Then all those who saw this miracle said, " This certainly is that prophet which Moses foretold would come into the world! " and they became so excited that they wanted to make Jesus king there and then.

It would have been fatal to his plans if the people had succeeded, for that would only have led to a revolution and war against the Romans. Jesus didn't want that, so he told the disciples to get into the boat and return to Capernaum, while he calmed the people and sent them home. When he had done this he went into the hills alone to pray.

The Bread of Life

IT WAS getting late when the disciples set out in their boat for Capernaum. As night fell a strong wind sprang up, and they were having a rough time on the water. For hours they rowed against the wind but seemed to get no further. Jesus, who was not with them, knew all about them, but he wanted them to learn that, though they could not always see him, he was still taking care of them. At last, about three o'clock in the morning, he went to them, walking across the water.

At first they thought it was a ghost moving on the waves, and they cried out with fear.

" Don't be afraid! " called Jesus to them. " It is I. Cheer up! "

When Peter saw who it was, he was so excited that he jumped up and shouted, " Lord, if it is you, let me come to you on the water."

" Come on, then," replied Jesus.

Peter jumped down out of the ship and began to walk on the waves; but when he saw how strong the wind was, he was afraid and began to sink.

" Save me, Lord," he cried.

Immediately Jesus stretched out his hand and caught him, saying, " How weak your faith is! Why did you begin to doubt? "

When they had both got into the boat, the wind and the waves dropped, and they soon reached the shore. The disciples were amazed that Jesus was able to walk on the water. " You really must be the Son of God himself! " they said.

The next morning the people who had been left behind could not understand why they were unable to find Jesus near Bethsaida, for they knew that he had not gone home with the disciples in the boat. When, at last, they came back to Capernaum and found Jesus already there they asked, " How did you get here? " But he would not tell them.

Already these crowds had spoilt the holiday that Jesus had planned for his disciples.

" You follow me about," he said, " only for what you can get, such as the free meal which I gave you. You ought not to worry so much about food that is gone when it is eaten, but about the food that will give you everlasting life."

" How should we do that? " they asked.

" You should believe in me whom God has sent," he replied.

" Well, what sign can you show us so that we can believe in you? " they asked. " Moses gave our fathers bread from heaven; what can you do? "

" Moses did not give you the bread of which I speak," said Jesus. " But my Father gives you the true bread from heaven which gives you life."

" Then, Lord," they replied, " give us this bread."

" I am the bread of life," said Jesus. " Whoever comes to me and believes in me shall never be hungry. But although you have seen me you don't believe in me."

The Jews began to grumble at this. " How can he say he is the bread that came down from heaven? This is Jesus whose mother and father we know. How can he say he came down from heaven? "

" He that believes in me," Jesus went on, " has everlasting life. That is why I say I am the bread of life. Your ancestors ate manna in the desert, but they are dead. I am the living bread that came down from heaven, and whoever eats this bread, that is to say whoever believes in me, shall live for ever. The bread that I give is my body, which I will give for the life of the world."

By this Jesus meant that by giving himself to die on the cross, he would die for the sins of the world, and so give everlasting life to all who accept him as their Saviour. The Jews could not understand this, so they said, " How can this man give us his body to eat? " and they took offence. Many of them deserted him, because they could not understand his sayings.

Walking across the wate

JESUS WITH HIS MEN

Avoiding Danger

I T WAS about the time of the Passover, and many of those who went up to Jerusalem told stories there of what Jesus was doing. Some of the scribes and Pharisees from Jerusalem therefore, went to Galilee to see for themselves. They were jealous of the crowds who followed Jesus, so they started finding fault again.

One of the rules which they had made up was that people must wash their cups and plates as well as their hands before a meal, because, whether they were dirty or not, they said everything was " unclean " until it was specially washed. The disciples took no notice of such silly rules, so the Pharisees took this opportunity to accuse them.

" Why do your disciples break the law," they asked Jesus, " by not washing before they eat? "

" Why do you cause people to break the commandments of God," asked Jesus in return, " by making up your own rules? Moses told you to honour your father and mother; but you have made it a law that if a man gives his money and services to God, it is no longer his duty to do any more for his parents. In that way you cancel out the laws of God by rules of your own invention.

" Listen," said Jesus, speaking to the people who had gathered round. " It is not that which goes into the mouth which harms a man, but that which comes out of it." He was referring to the false teaching which flowed from the mouths of the Pharisees.

Later on, when they reached home, his disciples asked him to tell them what he meant.

" Don't you see," explained Jesus, " that what you eat has no effect on your character, and can do you no real harm. It is from within, out of the heart, that evil comes: that is where evil thoughts, jealousy, pride and foolishness, begin. It is these things, which come from within, that defile a man."

The Pharisees had been very offended at what Jesus had said, but he had no desire to give them an opportunity to start further arguments. He had more important work to do training his disciples. So they set out on their long-promised holiday outside the Jewish province of Galilee in the district round Tyre and Sidon. Later, travelling round to the east of the Sea of Galilee, they went preaching and healing the sick in Decapolis. Once more crowds of people came to hear Jesus, and one day he fed more than four thousand of them on seven loaves and a few small fish.

To escape from the excited crowd he took ship across the lake with his disciples and landed near Magdala, some miles south of Capernaum. No sooner had they set foot again in the district of Galilee than the Pharisees were on to them once more.

" Show us a sign from heaven," they said, " so that we may know if you are the Christ."

" No sign shall be given you but the sign of Jonah," replied Jesus. " For as Jonah came back from the belly of the whale on the third day, so shall I return from the grave within three days."

Leaving them to puzzle out what that meant, Jesus and his disciples quickly got into their boat and crossed over to Bethsaida beyond Jordan. They had been in such a hurry to get away from the Pharisees that they had forgotten to buy bread, and found themselves with only one loaf. It was just as they discovered this that Jesus said, " You ought to be careful of the leaven of the Pharisees."

The disciples thought he meant the bread of the Pharisees, but when he saw that they had misunderstood him Jesus said, " Why worry because you have no bread? Have you already forgotten the five loaves that were enough for five thousand, and the seven loaves which satisfied four thousand? It is the teaching of the Pharisees which I call leaven, because of the way they spread it all over the country. Besides that, look how it makes them all puffed up with self-righteousness. That is why I warn you to have nothing to do with their teaching.

The Plan for Victory

WHEN they arrived at Bethsaida, Jesus took his disciples away into the rugged mountains and wooded valleys round Caesarea Philippi. There he could talk to them in peace without the interference of the Pharisees.

" Whom do people say that I am? " he asked them one day.

" Some say you are John the Baptist who has come to life again," they said. " Others think you are Elijah or one of the old prophets."

" But whom do you say that I am? " asked Jesus, coming to the point.

" You are the Christ," replied Peter, " the Son of the living God."

This was the answer for which Jesus had waited. " I thank God you know that," he said, " for by no human means could you have learned it. But that very knowledge shall be the foundation of my church."

Then he told them not to tell anyone else yet, for it would only make the priests accuse him of blasphemy.

Now that his disciples had learned to know that he was the Son of God, Jesus began to explain to them that he had not come to set up his kingdom by force in the way that everybody expected. He had once explained to Nicodemus that people are not fit for his kingdom as they are, but must first be born again with a new spirit. But because all men are sinners, all ought to die according to the law. Jesus made it clear that he alone, the Son of God who had not sinned, could die in the place of sinful men and bear the penalty of death for them, so that all who trust in him might have everlasting life.

" I must go up to Jerusalem," he told his disciples, " and must suffer many things at the hands of the chief priests. I shall even be killed, but I shall rise again on the third day."

The disciples could not understand this; they thought it was just another of his mysterious sayings.

" Surely," said Peter indignantly, " such things could never

Jesus was bathed in light

happen to you: you would never let them do it."

" Don't talk to me like that, you tempter! " said Jesus. " You don't understand the ways of God, but only the ways of men."

Turning to the others, Jesus went on, " If anyone wishes to follow me, he must follow my example and be willing to give up everything, even life itself, for the sake of what is right. Whoever prefers to save his life will only lose it; for what good would it do anyone if he had all the money in the world but lost his own soul?

" But," Jesus continued, " whoever is ashamed of me and of what I teach, of him shall I be ashamed when I come in the glory of my Father and with his angels. For I shall surely come again in glory and reward every man according to what he has done."

Then he made a wonderful promise to some of them: " There are some standing here," he said, " who shall see me in my glory before they die."

A week later he took Peter, James and John up a high mountain and began to pray. The three disciples soon fell asleep, for they were tired. When they woke up they saw a wonderful sight; Jesus was bathed in light, his face shining like the sun, while his clothes were glistening white. With him stood Moses and Elijah clothed in glory and speaking to Jesus about his coming death in Jerusalem.

" Master," said Peter, only half awake, " it is a good thing we are here. Let us put up three tents, one for you, one for Moses, and one for Elijah."

Just at that moment, however, a bright cloud came over them, and a voice from the cloud said, " This is my beloved Son: listen to him."

When the disciples heard this they were so frightened that they fell down and covered their faces, but Jesus came and touched them, saying, " Get up; don't be frightened! "

They looked up and Jesus was there alone.

" Tell no one," he said, " what you have seen until I am risen from the dead."

So they said nothing, but wondered what rising from the dead might mean.

The Power for Victory

THE NEXT morning, when Jesus came down from the mountain, he found a great crowd of people gathered round the disciples who had remained behind, and some scribes were asking questions. As soon as the people saw Jesus they came running towards him.

" What are you talking about? " Jesus asked.

One of the crowd came forward and explained: " Master, I have an only son who is possessed by an evil spirit. He suffers from terrible fits which throw him on the ground foaming at the mouth and grinding his teeth. I brought him to your disciples, but they could not cure him."

" You unbelieving people! " exclaimed Jesus. " How long must I put up with you. Bring your son to me."

As they were bringing the youth he went into yet another fit, rolling about on the ground.

" How long has he been having these fits? " asked Jesus.

" Ever since he was a child," replied the father. " Sometimes he is thrown into the fire or into the water. If you can do anything for him, have pity on us and cure him."

"*If!*" said Jesus. "Why, I can do anything, if only you believe I can."

" I do believe," cried the father with tears in his eyes. " Help me to believe more."

When Jesus saw that a crowd was gathering he spoke to the evil spirit: " Come out of him," he ordered, " and never go back."

Immediately the demon threw the boy into one last terrible fit and left him lying on the ground as if dead. Jesus took him firmly by the hand, lifted him up and led him to his father in his right mind.

Afterwards the disciples asked Jesus why they had not been able to drive this demon out.

" You have not enough faith," he replied. " This sort of demon will go out only after prayer."

After this they returned secretly to Capernaum, for there had been scribes in the crowd where the boy had been cured.

BACK IN JERUSALEM

The Jews who couldn't see

IT WAS autumn when Jesus returned to Capernaum, and many of the Jews were setting out to Jerusalem for the Feast of Tabernacles. His brothers, who did not believe in him, said to Jesus, " Why don't you leave these country places and go with us to Jerusalem and Judaea, where everybody can see the wonders you do? You can't expect to be known in public if you hide yourself away."

" It is not yet time for me to be known in public," replied Jesus. " Any time is good enough for you, because people don't hate you. But people hate me, because I show them what sinners they are. You go on up to the festival; I am not going up yet."

After his brothers had left, Jesus also went up to Jerusalem, travelling secretly by the short way through Samaria. Meanwhile everyone in Jerusalem was looking out for him. Halfway through the festival week Jesus surprised them all, when he suddenly appeared in the temple and began to teach.

" Isn't this the man they want to kill? " someone asked; " yet here he is speaking boldly in public, and nobody stops him."

" Perhaps," said another, " the priests have discovered that he really is the Christ after all."

" He can't be," added a third. " We know where this man comes from. When Christ comes we shan't know from where he comes."

" You think you know all about me," said Jesus, " and where I come from. But there is one who has sent me of whom you know nothing. I know Him, because He sent me. I shall only be with you a little while longer, and then I shall go back to Him who sent me. You will look for me, but will not find me, because you cannot come where I am going."

When they heard this many of the people believed that he came from God. " When Christ comes," they said, " surely he could never do more miracles than this man."

Others were angry and wanted to arrest him. " I can't see what he means," said one. "Where will he go where we can't find him? Does he mean to go and teach the tribes which are scattered among the nations? "

" I can't see how he can be the Christ," said another. " He comes from Galilee, but the prophet Micah said that the Christ would come from Bethlehem where David lived."

If only they had gone to Jesus, he could have shown them that although his mother had brought him up in Nazareth, she had been staying in Bethlehem when he was born.

When the Pharisees and chief priests heard what the people were saying about Jesus, they sent officers of the temple guard to arrest him. But when they came and heard what Jesus taught, they were afraid to touch him.

" We never heard anyone speak like this man," they said when they went back to report to the priests.

Meanwhile Jesus continued to teach in the temple. " I am the light of the world," he said. " Whoever comes to me will not be left in dark ignorance. If only you listen to what I say, you will be able to see the truth, and the truth will set you free."

" We are the children of Abraham," said the Jews proudly, " and were never the slaves of anyone. We can't see how you can set us free."

" Whoever sins," explained Jesus, " is unable to resist the temptation to sin again, so he becomes the slave of sin. The truth will set you free from sin, but if you do not believe who I am, you will die in your sins."

" Who are you, then? " they asked.

" When you have lifted me up, then you will know that I AM," replied Jesus, and he gave himself the name which God had spoken to Moses, when he spoke to him from the burning bush.

The Jews were outraged that Jesus should use this name; and when next day he claimed that he was God by using this name again, they took up stones to throw at him. Jesus, however, moved quietly into the crowd and left the temple.

The Blind Man who Could See

A S JESUS was leaving the temple he passed by a beggar who had been born blind.

"Master," said one of his disciples, "why was this man born blind? Was it because of his own sins or because of the sins of his parents?"

"It was neither because of his own sins nor those of his parents," answered Jesus. "Things like this are allowed to happen so that we may do God's work in helping those who suffer."

Jesus decided to leave the blind man to teach the unbelieving Jews a lesson: if only people would trust him, he would be able to help them to see, not only with their eyes, but with their minds as well.

"I am the light of the world," he told his disciples again. "So long as I am in the world, I must help those to see who cannot see."

Then Jesus spat on the ground and made clay with the dust and spittle. This he smeared over the eyes of the blind man, and told him to go and wash in the pool of Siloam. The blind man trusted Jesus enough to go and do what he was told, and as soon as he had washed in the pool he came back able to see.

His friends, and all those who knew that he had been blind, began to ask, "Isn't this the blind man who used to sit and beg?"

"Yes, it is," said some.

"No, it's not," said others, "but he looks very like him."

But the man himself told them, "I am the man who was blind."

"Well, how is it that you can see?" they asked.

"A man called Jesus made clay and put it on my eyes," he explained. "He told me to go to the pool of Siloam and wash. After I had gone and washed I could see."

"Where is this man?" they asked.

But he couldn't tell them.

After this they brought the man who had been blind to the Pharisees. Now it was the Sabbath day when Jesus had made clay

67

and restored the man's sight, so, of course, the Pharisees were very annoyed. They wanted to know exactly what Jesus had done.

" He put clay on my eyes," said the man, " and told me to go and wash. I did what I was told, and now I can see."

" He is evidently not a man of God," said some of the Pharisees, " because he doesn't keep the Sabbath."

Others asked, " How can a man who is a sinner do such miracles? " So there was an argument among them.

At length they turned to the blind man to get his opinion. " What do you think of this man who gave you your sight? "

" I think he's a prophet," replied the man simply.

The Jews wouldn't believe that. " I don't believe the man ever was blind," said one of them.

So they sent for the parents and asked them. " Is this your son who was born blind? "

" Yes, certainly," they answered. " He is our son, and he was born blind."

" Well, how is it," they asked, " that he can now see? "

Now his parents were afraid of the Jews, because they had said that if anyone admitted that Jesus was the Christ they would be turned out of the synagogue. So they said to the Pharisees, " We don't know how it is that he can see, or who gave him his sight. He is old enough to speak for himself; ask him."

The Jews, therefore, went back to the man who had been blind and said, " Tell us the truth, now: we know this man Jesus is a sinner."

" Whether he is a sinner or not," replied the man, " I don't know. All I know is that, whereas I was blind, now I can see."

" Well, what did he do to you? " they asked. " How did he restore your sight? "

" I have told you already," he answered, " but you would not listen. Why do you want to hear it all over again? Do you intend to become his followers? "

The Jews were furious at this cheeky question. " You may be

A beggar who had been born blind

one of that man's disciples yourself," they said, " but we are disciples of Moses. At least we do know that God spoke to Moses, but we don't know where this man comes from."

" Well, well, well! " said the man who was blind. " Isn't that marvellous? You don't know where he comes from, and yet he was able to give me my sight! Surely you know that God doesn't listen to sinners, but only to those who worship him and do his will. Since the world began, it has never been heard of that an ordinary man has given sight to one who was born blind. If this man were not from God he could do nothing."

" Who do you think you are? " asked the Jews, now more angry than ever. " You, who were born and bred in sin; who are you to teach us? Get out of here! " And they threw him out of the synagogue.

When Jesus heard that they had thrown him out, he sought him and asked, " Do you believe in the Son of God? "

" Who is he, Lord, that I might believe in him? " he asked.

" You have seen him," replied Jesus, " and it is I who am talking to you now."

" Lord, I do believe," he said; and he knelt at the feet of Jesus and worshipped him.

" I am the light of the world," said Jesus, noticing that some Pharisees were listening. " I have come into the world to help those who are blind to see, and to show those who think they can see, that they are blind."

" Are you saying that we are blind? " asked the Pharisees angrily.

" If you really were blind," replied Jesus, " I should not find fault with you; but since you say you can see, your sin remains."

A Famous Story

AFTER the Feast of Tabernacles Jesus went and taught in Peraea to the east of Jordan. One day there came to him one of the scribes, an expert on the law of Moses.

" Sir," he said, for he did not believe that Jesus was the Lord, but just another teacher, "sir, what must I do to receive everlasting life?"

" What does the law say? " asked Jesus; not because anyone can earn everlasting life by obeying the law, but because the law leads us to realise that we are all sinners, and until we know that we cannot be saved.

" Thou shalt love the Lord thy God with thy whole heart," replied the lawyer, " and thy neighbour as much as thyself."

" Quite right," said Jesus. " If you can do that you shall live."

" Well, who is my neighbour? " asked the lawyer, thinking he was able to keep this law and to love anyone if he tried.

So Jesus told him a story to show that not even the priests and Levites were able to keep the law.

" A man went down from Jerusalem to Jericho and was attacked by robbers who tore off his clothes, thrashed him and left him half dead by the roadside. Now it happened that a priest came along that way, but on seeing him there he passed by on the other side. Similarly a Levite saw him there but passed by on the other side.

"Finally a Samaritan travelling down the road saw him and took pity on him. He went and dressed his wounds, put him on his own ass and brought him to an inn and took care of him. Next day, when he left, he gave the innkeeper money, saying, ' Look after him, and if you have to spend anything more, I will pay you when I come this way again '.

" Now," said Jesus to the lawyer, " which of these three men would you say was a neighbour to the one who had been robbed? "

" The one who took pity on him," he replied.

" Quite right," said Jesus. "Now go and see if you can do that."

The Jews reject the Truth

IN THE winter Jesus returned to Jerusalem for the Feast of Dedication, and stayed the night at Bethany, a short distance from the city. Two sisters, Mary and Martha, lived there with their brother Lazarus, and they had invited Jesus to stay with them. Mary loved to sit at the feet of Jesus and listen to him, while Martha was busy getting the supper. Martha thought that Mary ought to help her, but Jesus said " No, it was just as important for her to listen to him."

Among the country folk Jesus had many such friends, but in Jerusalem he found his old enemies waiting for him. As soon as he went into the temple they came and questioned him again.

" How much longer are you going to keep us in doubt? " they asked. " If you are the Christ, tell us so plainly."

" I have told you so already," replied Jesus, " but you didn't believe me. You don't believe in me because you don't belong to my flock. My sheep listen to what I say, and I know them and they follow me. To them I give everlasting life, they shall never perish, neither shall anyone take them away from me. My Father who gave them to me is greater than all; no one can take them away from him, and I and my Father are one."

With these words Jesus gave them a plain answer to the question: " Are you the Christ? " But when the Jews heard this answer they took up stones to throw at him, showing that they would not believe in Jesus even when he told them the truth quite plainly.

" I have done many of my Father's good deeds for you to see," said Jesus. " For which one of them are you going to stone me? "

" We are not going to stone you for any good deed," they replied, " but for blasphemy, because you, being a man, make yourself out to be God."

" How is it," Jesus asked, " that you say of me, whom the Father has sent into the world, that I blaspheme when I say I am the Son of God? If I did not do the deeds of my Father you would not need

72

A Samaritan saw him

to believe in me; but if I do, you should accept the evidence of what I do. Then you would know and believe that the Father is in me."

After that they tried to arrest him, but he escaped from them, and went away again beyond Jordan to the place where John the Baptist used to preach.

It was not long, however, before some of the scribes and Pharisees from Jerusalem followed him. There they saw Jesus cure a dumb man who was possessed by an evil spirit. Here was one of those good deeds of which Jesus had spoken, and which he said proved that God was his heavenly Father.

The scribes and Pharisees, however, would not accept this evidence, but said, " He drives out demons by the power of Beelzebub, the prince of demons."

When Jesus heard this he put a question to them: " You say that I drive out demons by the power of Beelzebub. By whose power, may I ask, do your followers drive them out? Just go and ask them whether they can drive out demons by the power of the prince of demons; they will be able to tell you. But if a kingdom is divided and fights against itself it goes into ruin. So also if Satan is divided and fights against his own subjects his kingdom cannot stand. But if I cast out demons by the power of God, then surely the kingdom of God is here with you!

" You know full well the truth of this matter, yet you deliberately refuse to accept it. All kinds of sins shall be forgiven, but there is one kind of sin which shall never be forgiven, so I warn you that you are in danger of eternal damnation."

JEALOUS JEWS

A Victory over Death

WHILE Jesus was teaching in Peraea beyond Jordan, Lazarus fell ill. His sisters, Mary and Martha, were very worried because they thought he was going to die. Nothing they did for him seemed to do him any good at all.

" I think we ought to send for Jesus," said Mary. " He has cured so many sick people, I am sure he would have him well in no time."

" It's a bit late now," Martha replied. " It will be several days before we can fetch him; he is far away on the other side of the Jordan."

" All the more reason to hurry," urged Mary. " We'll send for him right away, and tell him to come as quickly as he can."

Lazarus lived with his sisters in Bethany near Jerusalem. It was quite a long way to the river Jordan, and Jesus was staying on the other side of the river. So the messenger had a long journey, and when at last he arrived he found that Jesus was very busy. A great many people were coming to listen to his teaching, while others waited to be cured of all their pains and sickness.

" Master," said the messenger, " your friend Lazarus is ill, and Mary and Martha are afraid he is going to die. Please come quickly and make him well."

" Don't worry," replied Jesus. " This illness will not end in death. It will be for the glory of God."

So Jesus went on teaching and healing for another two days. Suddenly he said to his disciples, " Let us go back to Bethany."

" But, Master," they cried, " you can't go back there so near to Jerusalem. The Jews who live there hate you and threw stones at you last time we were there."

" Are not twelve hours of daylight enough for our work? " asked Jesus. " We can keep a watchful eye on them during the day, and there will be no need to go out at night." Then he added, " Our

75

dear Lazarus is sleeping, but I will go and wake him."

" If he is sleeping he will soon be all right," said the disciples, still looking for an excuse not to go.

Jesus knew that he was really dead, though his friends thought he had meant natural sleep. So he told them plainly, " Lazarus is dead, but let us go to him."

The disciples were still afraid of the Jews, but Thomas said bravely, " We may as well all go and die together."

So Jesus and his disciples set off, but by the time they arrived in Bethany Lazarus had been dead and buried four days. Quite a number of friends had come to visit Mary and Martha to say how sorry they were that their brother had died. But as soon as Martha heard that Jesus was coming she went out to meet him on the road, while Mary remained in the house with her visitors.

When Martha saw Jesus she said, " Master, if only you had been here earlier I know you would have cured my brother and he would not have died. Even now I know that whatever you ask of God he will give it you."

" Your brother will rise again," said Jesus.

" I know," replied Martha, " and so shall we all on the last day."

" Yes," said Jesus. " All who believe in me shall rise again. They never really die, although the body goes to the grave. Do you believe that? "

" Oh yes, Lord," cried Martha, " and I believe that you are the Son of God who has come into the world to save us all." Then she ran off to fetch her sister Mary, telling her, " Jesus is here asking for you."

Mary ran quickly out of the house and down the road to meet him. When her friends who were with her saw her go, they, too, followed down the road. As soon as Mary met Jesus she fell down at his feet and cried, " Master, if only you had been here in time my brother would not have died."

When Jesus saw that Mary and her friends were all weeping because Lazarus was dead, he was deeply sorry for them and asked

Lazarus, come out !

quietly, " Where have you laid him? "

" Come and see," they replied, and they took him and showed him the cave where they had buried Lazarus. There was a large stone rolled in front of the entrance.

" Move away the stone," ordered Jesus.

At first they did not want to do this, but Jesus persuaded them and they moved the stone away.

Then, after giving thanks to God, Jesus called in a loud voice, " Lazarus, come out! "

The crowd gazed expectantly into the dark depths of the cave. Some knew of the great power of Jesus, because they had seen his miracles; some thought it would be too much to raise a corpse which had been dead four days; others laughed openly and thought the whole idea was ridiculous. All were struck with fear when they saw a white form heave itself forward out of the darkness.

The body had been bound up tightly hand and foot with bandages, and a white cloth was wound round the head and face.

" Untie him," said Jesus, " and set him free."

They did not need to be asked twice. Eager hands untied the bandages, and Lazarus was soon on his feet again and in good health. The tears of his friends were turned to shouts of joy as he returned home between his two sisters Mary and Martha.

When they saw this some of the Jews believed in Jesus, but others were angry, because they had been proved wrong about him. They went back to Jerusalem and told the priests and Pharisees that very soon everybody would follow Jesus, because he was able to do such wonderful things.

To the City of Doom

A S SOON as the rulers in Jerusalem heard about the raising of Lazarus they became very worried. They were afraid that the people would no longer listen to them, but would go and follow Jesus. So they immediately called together a secret meeting of all the priests and rulers of the people at the house of the High Priest.

" What are we going to do? " they asked. " This man Jesus is doing a great many miracles. Unless something is done, all the people will leave us and go and follow him."

" If this goes on," continued another, " they will soon be in open revolt against us. Unless something is done quickly they will make him king, and there may even be civil war."

" If there's a revolution," added a third, " the Romans will send an army which will destroy the temple and may even wipe out the whole nation."

" You don't know how to deal with this," said Caiaphas, the High Priest. " Surely it would be better that Jesus should die rather than that the whole nation should perish."

Little did he know that he was inspired by God to speak those words, and thus to declare that Jesus was to die to save the nation of Israel, and not only them, but all those who put their trust in him.

So they agreed that Jesus must be killed, and they made it known in the city that if anyone knew where he was he must tell the chief priests, and they would have Jesus arrested and put to death.

When he heard about this, Jesus left the neighbourhood of Jerusalem with his disciples and went away to a town on the border of the desert. But when the time of the great Feast of the Passover came round, the Jews began to look out for Jesus again. " What do you think? " they asked one another. " Do you think he will come up to the festival? "

A week before the Passover Jesus and his followers came back to Bethany and stayed there with Mary, Martha and Lazarus. This

79

news soon came to the ears of certain of the Jews in Jerusalem, and they planned to keep watch at the city gate and arrest him as soon as he entered. They would then take him to the chief priests and have him put to death.

While this plot was being hatched in Jerusalem Jesus and his disciples were having supper with Lazarus. As they were seated at the table Mary came and poured a bottle of costly perfume over his head and feet, so that the scent of it filled the whole house.

" What a waste! " said Judas Iscariot. " Why wasn't that perfume sold and the money given to the poor? " He said this not because he cared for the poor but because he kept the money-bag and used to steal from it.

" Leave her alone," replied Jesus; " it is a good deed which she has done. You can give money to the poor at any time, but she has done this in preparation for my burial. And I tell you this," he added, " wherever my story is told in the whole world, the deed that this woman has done shall also be told in memory of her."

This annoyed Judas very much, and he made up his mind from that time to join the enemies of Jesus.

The next day a great crowd of those who were going to the festival came to see Jesus and Lazarus, the man he had raised from the dead. Jesus sent into the next village for an ass and her foal, and when these were brought to him he mounted the foal and rode off towards Jerusalem, where the Jews were lying in wait for him at the gate.

The crowd was thrilled when they saw him riding the foal, because it was the custom in those days for a king to ride into the city on an ass when he was going to be crowned. Some of the people broke off branches of palm trees and waved them in the air in delight, while others took off their coats and laid them in the road for him to ride over. Amid the cheering crowd Jesus rode across the valley from Bethany to Jerusalem.

Everyone was delighted, but Jesus was feeling sad. " Poor Jerusalem! " he said to himself. " If only you knew what is coming to you! It will not be long now before your enemies besiege you and

81

She poured perfume over his feet

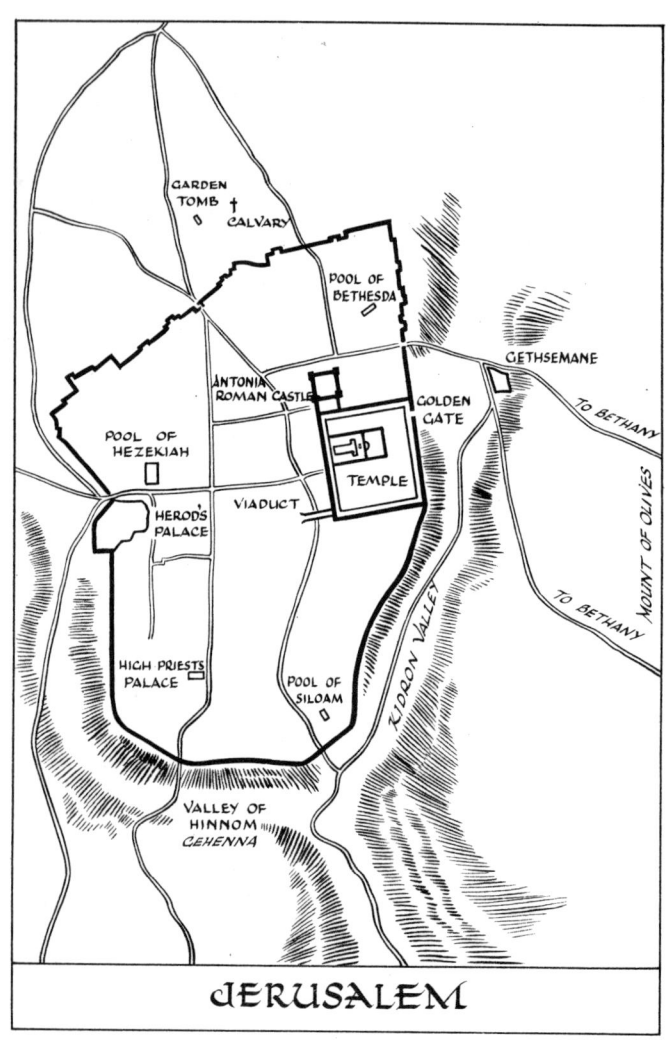

GARDEN
TOMB
CALVARY

POOL OF
BETHESDA

ANTONIA
ROMAN CASTLE

GETHSEMANE

TO BETHANY

GOLDEN
GATE

POOL OF
HEZEKIAH

TEMPLE

MOUNT OF OLIVES

VIADUCT

HEROD'S
PALACE

TO BETHANY

KIDRON VALLEY

HIGH PRIESTS
PALACE

POOL OF
SILOAM

VALLEY OF
HINNOM
GEHENNA

JERUSALEM

lay your walls level with the ground."

As they approached the gates of the city more people came out to greet him. They, too, were praising God for all the wonderful deeds he had done, and everybody was shouting " God save the king; the Son of David! Blessed is he who comes in the name of the Lord."

The Pharisees who had been waiting to arrest him at the city gate were very angry when they saw that Jesus was receiving this great welcome. They dared not go and take him prisoner at once, because they were afraid of all the people. " See how useless our plans are," they grumbled to one another. " The whole world is following him now."

So Jesus rode on quite safely into Jerusalem and came to the temple. There he found that the evil traders and money-changers were back again selling doves, lambs and cattle to those who needed them for sacrifices. As he had done once before, he drove out the traders and overturned the tables of the money-changers, scattering their coins on the ground. In the evening he left the city and returned to Bethany to stay the night with Mary and Martha.

Next morning he again went into Jerusalem and fearlessly drove the money-changers and traders out of the courtyard of the temple.

" My house shall be called a house of prayer," he said, " but you have made it a den of thieves."

When the priests saw this they were more furious than ever, but they dared not arrest him, because of all the people who followed him.

THE FINAL CONTEST

A Battle of Words

TWO DAYS later, as Jesus was teaching and curing the sick in the temple, a party of priests and rulers of the people came and asked, " What right have you to come here and do these things? "

" You tell me first," replied Jesus, " what right had John the Baptist to preach? Was his message from God or from man? "

This was a very difficult question for them to answer. If they said it was from God, then Jesus would ask them why they did not believe him when he said that Jesus was the Christ, the Son of God. If they said it was from man, they would be afraid of all the people who believed in John.

So the priests replied, " We cannot say."

" Very well," answered Jesus, " neither will I say by what right I do these things.

" And now you tell me what you think of this story," he went on. " A certain man planted a vineyard and put it in charge of vine-dressers while he went away for a long time to a distant country. When the time came for the fruit to be ripe he sent his servants to fetch some of it from the vine-dressers. But the vine-dressers beat one, killed another and threw stones at a third. So the owner sent more servants, but these they treated in the same way. Finally he sent his only son, saying, Surely they will take notice of my son.

" But when the vine-dressers saw the son, they said, ' This is the heir: let's kill him and then the vineyard will be ours.' So they caught him and killed him and threw him out.

" Now tell me," said Jesus, " when the owner of the vineyard comes, what should he do to those vine-dressers? "

" He should put the miserable wretches to death," said the priests, " and then put the vineyard in charge of decent vine-dressers who will let him have his fruit when it is ripe."

84

Jesus told them about his kingdom

" Quite right," answered Jesus. " And therefore I say to you that the kingdom of God shall be taken from you and given to another nation which shall produce the fruits of it."

When the chief priests and Pharisees heard this they realised that when Jesus had spoken of the vine-dressers' behaviour, he had been referring to the way in which the Jews had treated God's prophets all down the ages. They also knew that Jesus claimed to be God's Son. He had thus led them to condemn their own actions, and in their anger they would have liked to kill him on the spot, but they were afraid to do it because of the people.

It was not long before one of them thought of an idea to get rid of the people. Calling some Roman soldiers as witnesses, they tried to lay a trap for Jesus.

" Master," they said, " we know that you are an honest man and teach the way of God without regard to what anyone says. Tell us now, is it right to pay taxes to Caesar? "

The idea was that if Jesus said Yes he would lose the friendship of the people who prevented his arrest, for no one liked paying taxes, least of all the Jews to their Roman overlords. If, on the other hand, Jesus said No, then the Roman soldiers were witnesses that he had forbidden the people to pay taxes to Caesar.

Jesus saw through this at once. " Why do you try to catch me? " he asked. " Show me some of the tax money. Now," he went on when they had produced some coins, " whose head and name is on them? "

" Caesar's," they replied.

" Very well," said Jesus. " If you use Caesar's money you must pay his taxes. Give to Caesar the things which are Caesar's, and to God the things which are God's."

His friends were very pleased with this wise reply, but the Pharisees were amazed and angry at the ease with which he had avoided their trap.

So the battle of words went on as Jesus taught each day in the temple court, returning each night to stay with his friends in Bethany.

Jesus attacks the Pharisees

AFTER a time the Pharisees grew tired of asking Jesus questions; his answers were not always to their liking. So Jesus turned and spoke to the crowds who filled the temple court.

" You want to be careful of the scribes and Pharisees," he began. " They have the law at their finger-tips, so you had better do what they tell you; but don't follow their example, for they do little more than talk. They make rules and pass laws which make life a burden to everyone, but they never do anything to make life easier."

This was just what the people liked to hear; rules are always a nuisance, and they were tired of them.

" Everything the Pharisees do," Jesus went on, " is just the opposite of how the people of my kingdom behave. Look how they dress themselves up in fine clothes and sit in the front seats in the synagogue where they can be admired. They always want the best places at a party, and in the street they like to be called ' master.'

" You should have no wish to be called master, for you have only one Master who is Christ, and you are all equal. Nor should you want to make yourselves important, for whoever wants to make himself important shall be the least in the kingdom of heaven."

Seeing some of his enemies standing at the back of the crowd, Jesus began to attack them: " As for you scribes and Pharisees," he continued, " you cannot possibly enter the kingdom of heaven yourselves; all you can do is to prevent others from coming in. Even if you scour the whole world to make one convert, when you have got him you make him twice as bad as yourselves."

Such plain speaking had not been heard in the temple for many long years, but Jesus had not finished yet.

" A curse on you scribes and Pharisees," he cried. " You split hairs over taxes and quibble over rules, while all the time you neglect the really important matters of the law, such as justice, mercy and fair play. You make a fuss about the washing of cups and plates, while your own hearts and minds are full of cheating and greed."

This was just what the poor people had thought for a long time, but no one had dared to complain. Now that Jesus was boldly showing up the wickedness of their rulers on the steps of the temple itself the crowd were with him, and the Pharisees were powerless to stop him.

" Yes, you are the people," Jesus went on, " who have built grand tombs and memorials to the prophets of God, whom your own fathers have put to death. How can such a miserable lot of worms escape the punishment of hell? "

After this attack on the Pharisees, Jesus left the temple and made his way with the disciples to the Mount of Olives.

It was not long, of course, before the chief priests and rulers heard what Jesus had been saying about the scribes and Pharisees to the crowds in the temple court. They called a meeting at once of all the chief priests and rulers, and when these had gathered in the palace of Caiaphas, the High Priest, they began to discuss what they could do to stop Jesus. Somehow, they said, he must be arrested and put to death as soon as possible. They decided, however, not to do this on the feast day, for they were afraid it might cause a riot among the people.

While this meeting was going on Judas Iscariot made up his mind to offer to betray Jesus to his enemies. Secretly he went to the chief priests and said, " What will you give me if I show you how you can arrest Jesus when he is alone? "

This was just what the priests and rulers were waiting for, so they offered to pay Judas thirty pieces of silver. From that time he kept watch for an opportunity to betray Jesus when the people were not with him.

The Last Supper

ON THE first day of the festival Peter and John came and asked Jesus where he was going to eat the Passover supper. This was just what Judas would like to know. If he could tell the chief priests this, they could send some soldiers to arrest Jesus and all his disciples at once when there were no crowds of people to protect them. But Jesus was not giving the secret away.

" Go into Jerusalem," he said to Peter, " and there you will see a man carrying a pitcher of water. Follow him to whatever house he goes, and say to the man who lives there, ' Where is your guest-room? The Master wishes to eat the Passover in your house with his disciples.' The man will then show you a large upper room; that is where I want you to get the supper ready."

Peter and John did as Jesus told them, and found the man carrying a pitcher. This was an unusual sight, because in Jerusalem only women carry water in pitchers; the men use water-skins. Peter and John followed the man home, and arranged with the landlord to let them have the upstairs room for the Passover supper that night.

So instead of returning to Bethany that evening, Jesus stayed in the city after dark, without giving Judas the chance to let the chief priests know where he was.

When his twelve disciples had gathered for the meal, Jesus said to them, " I am glad that I have been able to eat this supper with you, for it will be the last time I shall do so until we meet in the kingdom of God."

As the disciples were taking their places at the table they began to argue among themselves about who should have the best seats, and who was the youngest; for it was the duty of the youngest to act as servant and wash the dust of the road from the others' feet.

Jesus was sad to find that, after all he had taught them, his disciples still understood so little about the way people should behave in his kingdom. Rising from the table, he took off his long outer garment, tied a towel round his waist and poured out a basin full of water. Then he began to wash the disciples' feet, drying them with the towel which he had round him.

Already Peter was very ashamed that his Master should have to do this humble task. When it was his turn he said, " Surely, Lord, you are not going to wash my feet! "

" You may not know what I am doing now," replied Jesus, " but afterwards you will understand."

" Never," Peter insisted, " will I allow you to wash my feet."

" If I don't wash you," Jesus said, " it means that you will have nothing to do with me."

" In that case," answered Peter, " wash not only my feet but my hands and head as well."

" Anyone who has had a bath," replied Jesus, " needs to have only his feet washed, and he is clean all over. And you people are all clean except one." Jesus said " except one," because he knew that one of them, Judas Iscariot, was a traitor.

After he had washed their feet and put on his garments again, Jesus sat down and said, " Do you know what I have done?

" You call me Master and Lord, and quite rightly, for so I am. If I, then, your Lord and Master, wash your feet, as if I were a servant, you also ought to treat one another likewise. I have set you an example to show you how you ought to behave; let him that is greatest among you be as the youngest, and he that is chief be as the servant.

" The kings and rulers of the nations order their people about and tell them what they have got to do. But in my kingdom it will not be like that. Everyone will do willingly whatever needs to be done without being ordered about. Once you know this, and act on it by doing things for one another, you will have learnt the secret of happiness."

Betrayed

FOR SOME days now Jesus had been saying strange things which his friends did not understand. Now he gave them a terrible shock: " You know," he said, " that in the Psalm it is foretold that 'one who eats bread at my table will turn and kick me.' Therefore I warn you now before it actually happens this evening, so that when it does happen you will know and believe that I am the Christ."

Then he said to them very solemnly, " I tell you that this very night one of you will betray me."

At this his disciples gazed anxiously from one to another, wondering who it could be. " Master, who is it? " they asked. " Is it I? "

" It is one of you twelve," replied Jesus, " who is eating at the table with me."

That did not satisfy Peter, so he made a sign to John who was sitting next to Jesus: " Find out whom he means," he said.

Jesus whispered, " It is the one to whom I shall pass this piece of bread." And he passed it to Judas Iscariot.

At that moment Judas realised that this was just the opportunity for which he had been waiting.

" What you are about to do," said Jesus to him, " do quickly." The others at the table did not know what this meant. If they had known, they would never have let Judas go; but as it was, they thought that perhaps he had to go and buy something. Quickly, before they realised what his terrible errand was, he rose from the table and went out into the night to tell the High Priest where Jesus could be found.

When he had gone Jesus took bread and broke it, giving it to his disciples, saying, " This is to represent my body which I am giving for you: eat this in memory of me."

After supper he took the cup of wine and gave it to them, saying, " Drink this in memory of me, for it represents my blood given to seal the New Covenant."

So it has always been from that day that Christians have broken

Gethsemane

bread and drunk wine in memory of the one who died for their sins.

Later, as they made their way out of the city in the direction of the Mount of Olives, Jesus spoke to Peter.

" Satan has been allowed to tempt all of you this night," he said, " but I have prayed for you specially, that your faith will not fail. Afterwards I want you to help the others to keep up their faith."

" Lord, I am willing to go with you even to prison or to death," boasted Peter.

" This night," explained Jesus, " all of you will turn against me and desert me; but after I am risen I will meet you in Galilee."

" Desert you! " cried Peter. " I will never desert you."

" It is true," replied Jesus, " that this very night, before the cock crows twice, you will yourself disown me three times."

" I would rather die," declared Peter, " but I will never disown you." And all the others said the same.

Soon after this they came to the Garden of Gethsemane, which was near the road to Bethany in the Kidron valley. This was a favourite place for them to visit, and one which was also known to Judas. There Jesus left some of his disciples and went on a little way by himself to pray for strength and courage to face the terrible ordeal which he knew was coming. The hour was late, and twice he returned to find his friends were sleeping. Each time he woke them and returned to pray.

Meanwhile Judas had been to the High Priest, who sent out a party of soldiers and temple police to arrest Jesus. Judas was leading them along the Kidron valley to the garden where he knew he would find Jesus. The soldiers were all armed and carried lanterns and torches. Judas had arranged with them a sign that he would go and kiss the one who was to be arrested.

It must have been about midnight when Jesus finished praying. He returned again to find his friends asleep, but he woke them, saying, " We must be going. My betrayer is close at hand."

With great courage he went forward to meet those who were moving through the dark shadows in search of him. Suddenly Judas, who was leading, came forward and kissed him; then, as the soldiers followed, Jesus asked them, " Whom are you looking for? "

" For Jesus of Nazareth," they answered.

" I am he," he replied.

The soldiers fell back in surprise, so Jesus asked them once more, " Whom do you want? "

" Jesus of Nazareth," they said.

" I have told you that I am he," replied Jesus. " If you are looking for me, let these friends of mine go their way."

As the soldiers stepped forward again to arrest him, Peter drew his sword and, aiming at the servant of the High Priest, cut off his right ear.

"Put back your sword," said Jesus; " do you not suppose that if I required it, my Father would instantly send me twelve legions of angels? But I must go through with what the Father has given me to do." With that he touched the man's ear with his hand, and he was healed.

Turning to the crowd of soldiers, Jesus asked, " Have you come out with swords and sticks as if to fight a robber? Day after day I have been sitting in the temple and you did not dare to lay hands on me."

Then he gave himself up to them, and they bound him and took him away to the High Priest.

As they led Jesus away all his friends deserted him and fled. When they saw that he was being taken towards the city they went in the opposite direction towards Bethany, where they were lodging. But Peter and John did not return all night, and the others thought that they must have been arrested along with Jesus. All the next day they were afraid to go into Jerusalem lest the Jews should take them captive as well.

THE TRIAL

Denied by a Friend

PETER and John had quickly recovered from the shock of the arrest of their Master. They wanted to see all that was going to happen, and to be at hand if he required their help. So instead of running away to Bethany they followed at a distance behind the soldiers, and saw them take Jesus into the palace of the High Priest.

John, who was known to the High Priest, followed them, but Peter stayed outside till John asked the maid at the door to let him in.

But the maid asked Peter, "Aren't you one of this man's followers?"

" No, I am not," replied Peter: and the maid let him go into the courtyard. There a number of the servants and police were lighting a fire. It was cold, so Peter went to join them and warmed himself, while John went into the palace to see what was happening to Jesus.

Annas, who was father-in-law of Caiaphas, the High Priest, was asking Jesus questions about his disciples and teaching.

" I have never made any secret of my teaching," said Jesus, " but have always taught in the synagogue and temple and other public places where the Jews assemble. But why are you questioning me? You ought to ask those that heard me what it was that I taught: there are witnesses who know what I said."

This put Annas in the wrong, because, according to Jewish law, accusations had to be made by the witnesses and not by those who were trying the case. Nevertheless, one of the officers who was standing near struck Jesus a blow and asked, " Is that the way to talk to a chief priest? "

" If I have said anything wrong," replied Jesus, " prove it. But if not, why hit me? "

After this Annas handed Jesus over to Caiaphas, the High Priest, who by this time had called together a hurried meeting of the Sanhedrin, which was the Jewish court of justice. Now Caiaphas had already made up his mind that Jesus must at all costs be put to

Peter went out and wept

death, but it was not easy for him to bring this about, because the Romans did not allow the Jewish court to condemn anyone to death. If the Jews found anyone guilty of a crime for which he ought to die, then they had to bring the prisoner before Pontius Pilate, the Roman governor. Consequently his purpose was to find evidence against Jesus on which Pilate would condemn him to death.

At first Caiaphas tried to bring false witnesses who would give evidence on which Jesus could be condemned. But although there were many who gave false evidence, they did not agree together in what they said; and unless they agreed their evidence could not be accepted according to their law. So Jesus stood silent before them, for there was no case to be answered.

Meanwhile Peter was standing outside in the courtyard warming himself by the fire when a maid-servant of the High Priest said, " Surely, you were with Jesus of Nazareth? "

" I don't know him," replied Peter. " I don't know what you are talking about."

Then someone else said, " You are one of them."

As Peter denied his Lord for the third time that night, the cock crew once.

About an hour later another maid noticed him and told those who stood by, " This fellow was also with Jesus."

" I don't know the man," said Peter.

Then one of those who had taken part in the arrest recognised him and asked, " Didn't I see you with him in the garden? " But again Peter denied it.

" Surely, you must be one of them," added another. " You speak with a Galilaean accent."

" I tell you I know nothing about the man," said Peter angrily; and even as he spoke, he heard the cock crow a second time. At that moment the Lord turned and looked at him, and he remembered what Jesus had said: " Before the cock crows twice, you will disown me three times."

Ashamed, he went out and wept bitterly.

Before the Sanhedrin

ALL THIS time the High Priest was bringing witnesses to try to convict Jesus of some crime. At last one came who declared that Jesus had said, " I am able to destroy the temple of God and to build a new one in three days."

Then another witness claimed that Jesus had said, " I will pull down this temple built by human hands, and in three days I will erect another built without hands."

These two reports certainly agreed very closely with one another, and with what Jesus had really said, namely, " If you destroy this temple I will raise it up in three days." But he had been speaking of the temple of his body, and meant that if he were killed he would come to life again within three days. This, he said, was to be the sign by which people might know that he was the Christ, the Son of God.

Caiaphas realised, however, that Pilate was not likely to condemn Jesus to death merely for making a claim that he could rebuild the temple in three days. Such a charge would be laughed out of court. So he said that, because these two witnesses did not agree exactly, their charge was no good. Then he went on trying to discover other witnesses who would bring a more serious charge, but he could find none.

At length the High Priest rose to his feet and, addressing Jesus, asked, " Have you no answer to make? What have you to say to all this evidence which has been brought against you? "

Still Jesus made no reply. Since none of the witnesses had agreed together, there was no case to answer.

Then the High Priest said, " I ask you, in the name of the living God, to tell us whether you are the Christ, the Son of God."

" Yes, I am," answered Jesus at last, " and I tell you that one day you will see me at the right hand of Divine power, coming in the clouds of heaven."

If the High Priest had been conducting the trial in a proper manner he ought at least to have asked Jesus for evidence that his claim was true. Instead he assumed that it was a lie, and, turning to the assembly, exclaimed, " Blasphemy! Now you have heard him yourselves. What further need have we of witnesses? What is your verdict? "

" He must die," they all declared.

At that they began to spit in his face, then they blindfolded him, and struck at him with their fists and hands, saying, " If you are a prophet, tell us who it was that hit you." So they made fun of Jesus and bullied him till break of day.

At dawn all the elders and rulers of the people met together with the chief priests and scribes to discuss what they would do with him, for they were not allowed to put anyone to death without the consent of the Roman governor. Jesus was brought before this assembly, and again they asked him, " Are you the Christ? "

" Even if I were to tell you," he replied, " you would not believe me. But after this I shall be seated at God's right hand of power."

" You are the Son of God, then? " they cried.

" Yes," he answered, " I am."

" Then we have no need of further evidence," they declared. " We have heard it from his own lips."

So the whole assembly rose and took him to Pontius Pilate, the Roman governor, and began to accuse him.

When Judas Iscariot, who had betrayed him, saw that Jesus was about to be condemned to death he was bitterly sorry for what he had done. Taking the thirty pieces of silver, he went to the chief priests and said, " I did wrong in betraying to death one who is innocent."

" What has that to do with us? " they replied. " That is your affair."

But Judas flung down the money in the temple and went out and hanged himself.

None of the witnesses agreed

Before Pontius Pilate

IT was still very early in the morning when Jesus was taken bound through the city to the Roman governor. The chief priests waited outside with their prisoner, because they would not enter a heathen judgment hall during the festival, lest they should be regarded as unclean, and no longer be allowed to partake of the feast.

Because they would not go in, Pontius Pilate, the Roman governor, came out to them on the pavement and asked, " What charge do you bring against this man? "

The Jews had not expected that Pilate would ask them this. They only wanted to get his permission to put Jesus to death.

" If this man were not a criminal," they replied, " we would not have brought him to you."

" Well, in that case," said Pilate, " take him and judge him according to your own law."

" But we are not allowed to put anyone to death," replied the priests.

It was becoming clear to them that things were not going as they had planned. Pilate was evidently going to insist on a proper trial before he sentenced Jesus to death. Further, if he knew that Jesus had been convicted only for blasphemy he would certainly not allow him to die for it, because the Romans were heathen. For this reason, the Jews were obliged to make fresh charges and bring more false evidence to obtain a conviction under the Roman law.

The chief priests, therefore, began to accuse Jesus of some new crime, saying, " We found this fellow perverting the nation, and forbidding the people to pay tribute to Caesar. He says that he himself is the king."

They accused him falsely, not only of this but of many other things, but all the time Jesus stood silent and made no reply in self-defence.

At last Pilate turned to him and said, " Have you nothing to say in answer to all these charges which are brought against you?"

Still Jesus spoke no word, at which the governor was astonished. So he went into the judgment hall and sent for Jesus privately, while the Jews remained outside.

" Are you king of the Jews? " asked Pilate.

" Do you ask this yourself," queried Jesus, " or are you enquiring what others have said about me? "

" I am enquiring about what your own people and the chief priests say," explained Pilate. " What is it that you have done? "

" My kingdom," replied Jesus, " is not of this world; if my kingdom were of this world, then my servants would have fought for me to prevent my being taken captive by the Jews: but my kingdom is not here."

" You are a king, then? " asked Pilate.

" Yes, I am," said Jesus. " For this purpose I was born, and for this cause I came into the world."

Having satisfied himself that Jesus had made no rival claim to the Roman Emperor, the governor rose and went out again to the people. There he found that an angry mob had joined the chief priests and rulers.

When he had obtained silence he announced, " I find no fault in this man."

For a moment the priests were dumb. Pilate had acquitted their prisoner, and was evidently about to set him free. This would never do, so at once they renewed their accusations more loudly than ever, shouting, " He has been stirring up the people with his teaching throughout all Judaea—even from Galilee, where he started, to this place."

Pilate could see that the crowd would soon get out of control, and he feared that there would be a riot if he released Jesus. So when he heard that Jesus came from the district of Galilee he asked, " Is this man a Galilaean, then? "

" Yes," the people cried. " He comes from Nazareth in Galilee."

" Then you should take him to Herod, the governor of Galilee," replied Pilate. He was glad to find any excuse to be rid of this difficult case.

Now it happened that Herod was in Jerusalem at that time, so the priests immediately set off across the city to bring Jesus before him. Herod was very pleased that Pontius Pilate had allowed him to hold court in Judaean territory. He was even more glad to have the opportunity of meeting Jesus, for he had heard a great deal about him, and had for a long time wished to see him perform some of his wonderful miracles. But when Herod asked him questions about who he was, Jesus made no reply.

" Are you John the Baptist," said Herod, " who, as some say, has risen from the dead? "

Jesus gave no answer.

" He says he is king of the Jews," called the priests, " and he is stirring up the people with his teaching."

" So you call yourself a king, do you? " sneered Herod, annoyed because Jesus would not answer him. " I don't think you look much like a king. Let us see what you would look like in royal robes."

So Herod and his soldiers dressed Jesus in a gorgeous costume and made fun of him. But he would not allow Jesus to be put to death, because he thought that his claim to be king of the Jews was too ridiculous. So when he was tired of making fun of Jesus he sent him back to Pontius Pilate with the message that he had found that Jesus had done nothing worthy of death.

Pilate was astonished

Condemned to Death

WHILE the priests had been accusing Jesus before Herod, Pilate had received a message from his wife, saying, "Have nothing to do with that innocent man, for I have just had a terrible dream about him." This worried him, and when the chief priests and rulers of the people had brought Jesus back, and the crowd had again gathered outside the Roman judgment hall, Pilate addressed them once more.

"You have brought this man to me," he said, "on a charge of stirring up rebellion among the people. I have examined him, and found no cause for the accusations which you bring against him; no, neither does Herod, for he has sent him back to me. So, you see, he has done nothing which deserves death. But it is a custom at the Passover for me to release to you one prisoner. I shall therefore have this man whipped and release him."

At this the whole crowd roared in anger, "Away with him! Not this man but Barabbas." Barabbas was a man who had been imprisoned for murder and for causing a riot.

Pilate, however, knew that the priests had only brought their accusations against Jesus because they were jealous of him. He wanted to release Jesus, so he asked the people again, "Whom shall I set free: Barabbas or Jesus?"

But the people, led by the priests, shouted for Barabbas.

Once more Pilate asked them, "What shall I do, then, with Jesus who is called the Christ?"

With one voice they cried, "Crucify him! Crucify him!"

"But what crime has he committed?" pleaded Pilate. "I have found nothing in him worthy of death."

Still the people continued to shout wildly, "Crucify him! Crucify him!"

Above the uproar Pilate could no longer make himself heard. He was afraid that a riot might break out at any moment, but he refused to have a hand in the crucifixion of Jesus. He called for a basin of water, and in the sight of all the people he washed his hands, saying, " I will have nothing to do with this bloodshed. I wash my hands of it: it is your responsibility."

" His blood shall be on us and on our children! " cried all the people.

Pilate was determined to carry out his purpose, so he sent Jesus to be whipped, intending to set him free afterwards. The Roman soldiers took Jesus away, stripped him of his clothes and flogged him. Then they put a scarlet robe on him, and made a crown of thorns and put it on his head. They put a cane in his right hand as a sceptre, and knelt before him in jeering fun, crying, " Hail, king of the Jews! "

Then they spat upon him and, taking the cane from him, beat him repeatedly on the head. At last, their cruel sport over, they brought him back to Pilate, who led him out before the people still dressed in the scarlet robe and wearing the crown of thorns.

" Look! " said Pilate. " I am bringing him out to you. Please understand that I find no fault in this man."

But as soon as the chief priests and rulers saw Jesus they madly took up their cry of, " Crucify him! Crucify him! "

" Then take him yourselves and crucify him," said Pilate defiantly. " I, at any rate, find no fault in him."

The priests, were not anxious to take the whole responsibility on themselves. " We have a law," they said, " and according to that law he ought to die, because he called himself the Son of God."

Pilate became more alarmed than ever at this. He had Jesus taken once more into the judgment hall and began to question him. " Who are you," he asked, " and where do you come from? "

Jesus gave him no answer.

" Will you not answer me? " said Pilate sharply. " Do you not realise that I have it in my power to release you or to crucify you? "

" You would have no power over me at all," replied Jesus, " unless it were given you from above. So he who has delivered me up to you is more guilty than you are."

When he heard this, Pilate was more determined than ever to let

Jesus go free.

Leaving him in the judgment hall, he went out again to tell the people that he would set Jesus free. His efforts were in vain, however, for the Jews continued to shout that Jesus should be put to death.

" Anyone who sets himself up as king is an enemy of Caesar," someone shouted. " If you let this man go you are no friend of Caesar's."

This was a crafty move. Pilate saw at once what was meant. If he released Jesus it would be reported to the Emperor that he had sided with a rebel and enemy of Caesar. He would probably be recalled to Rome to answer this charge, and evidence would be brought that Jesus had claimed to be king. How could he explain that Jesus was no leader of a rebellion against Rome?

In one last effort to show the Jews that they would be telling a lie if they gave such evidence against him, Pilate brought Jesus out before them and asked them, " If you make this man out to be a rebel leader, here he is: go and make him your king! "

It was no use. " We don't want him! " they shouted. " Take him away and crucify him! "

" Shall I crucify your king, then? " asked Pilate sarcastically.

" We have no king but Caesar! " they answered.

It was clear that these Jews, who really hated having Caesar as their ruler, would tell any number of lies to get Pilate into trouble if he set Jesus free. He feared that he might be convicted and possibly condemned to death if he released Jesus, so Pilate, in order to save himself, gave way.

" Very well, then," he replied. " Take your king and crucify him." And he ordered Barabbas to be released.

They made a crown of thorns

THE LAST SACRIFICE

Crucified

THE FLOGGING that Jesus had received at the hands of the Roman soldiers had been a terrible ordeal. Many a man had died under such punishment. When they led Jesus away to crucify him he was too exhausted to carry his cross all the way, and they forced a passerby, named Simon, a Cyrenian, to carry it.

As they made their way through the narrow streets of the city to Calvary, a hill just outside the northern wall, a great crowd of people followed, many of them women, weeping and mourning for him.

Turning to them, Jesus said, " Daughters of Jerusalem, do not weep for me, but weep rather for yourselves and your children. For a time is coming when women will wish that they had never had children. They will cry to the mountains to fall on them, and the hills to cover them up. If they do such things as this while I am here, what will they do when I have gone? "

Two criminals who were robbers were also brought out of the city with Jesus. When they reached Calvary they offered the three who were to be crucified wine mixed with gall, a drink which would lessen the pain. But as soon as he had tasted what it was Jesus refused to take it.

The soldiers then nailed Jesus to the cross, and the two robbers as well, setting up their crosses one on the right and the other on the left. Yet even as the soldiers drove the nails through his hands and his feet Jesus prayed for them, saying, " Father, forgive them, for they know not what they are doing."

Pilate had given orders that a notice should be fixed to the cross, saying in Hebrew, Latin and Greek:
THIS IS JESUS OF NAZARETH, KING OF THE JEWS.

When the chief priests had seen this they were very annoyed and complained to Pilate. " Don't put ' King of the Jews '," they said, " but put ' He said I am king of the Jews '."

Simon, a Cyrenian

But Pilate would not listen, and answered, " What I have written, I have written."

As soon as the soldiers had crucified Jesus they took his clothes and divided them into four parts, one for each of them. But the coat had no seam, being woven in one piece from top to bottom, so they said, " Don't let's tear it to pieces, but we will draw lots for it."

Meanwhile the chief priests and all those who passed by sneered at Jesus as he hung there on the cross.

" You said you could pull down the temple," they called, " and build a new one in three days; now show us if you can come down off the cross."

The soldiers also joined in, laughing and saying, " If you are king of the Jews, save yourself."

In the same way the priests and rulers of the people jeered at him. " He saved others," they said, " but he cannot save himself. If he is king of Israel, let him come down from the cross now, and we will believe him. He trusted in God that he would deliver him: let him deliver him now, for he claims to be the Son of God."

Even one of the robbers who was crucified with him began to insult him. " If you are the Christ," he said, " save yourself and us as well."

But the other replied, " Don't you even fear God when you are suffering the same punishment with him? We, indeed, are suffering justly, for we are being punished for the crimes we have done. But this man has done nothing wrong." Then, speaking to Jesus, he added, " Remember me when you come into your kingdom."

" I tell you in truth," replied Jesus, " that this very day you will be with me in paradise."

Among those in the crowd who had come out from Jerusalem were John and the mother of Jesus with her sister, also Mary, the wife of Cleopas, and Mary Magdalene. As they stood near the foot of the cross Jesus knew how his mother would feel the loss of her son, so he said to her, " Look, take John to be your son." And to John he said, " Take her to be your mother." So John took her and looked after her in his own home.

About midday there came a strange darkness over the whole land, and this lasted until about three o'clock in the afternoon. Then Jesus suddenly cried out in a loud voice, " My God, my God, why hast thou forsaken me? "

Some of those who stood by thought that he was calling on Elijah to come and help him. But a moment later, knowing that the end had come, he said, " I am thirsty."

There was a jar of wine standing there, so one of them dipped a sponge in it, and passed it up to Jesus on the end of a stick, saying, " Let us see whether Elijah will come and take him down."

When he had tasted the wine he said, " It is finished."

A moment later he called again in a loud voice, " Father, into thy hands I give my spirit," and with those words he died.

Immediately the earth shook and the rocks split; in the temple the veil of the sanctuary was torn from top to bottom. The soldiers who were standing guard by the crosses were terrified.

" This man was surely innocent," their captain exclaimed in alarm. " He was surely the Son of God."

The crowds who had come to see the sight returned to the city weeping and mourning for Jesus, who had been so kind and done so many good deeds for them. But Mary Magdalene and the wife of Cleopas and some of his friends who had come from Galilee remained standing at a distance still looking on.

Dead and Buried

WHEN the Jews saw that Jesus was dead they went to Pilate and asked that the three bodies might be removed before sunset, because they did not want them to remain on the crosses during the Sabbath. Pilate, therefore, gave orders that the legs of the dying men should be broken to hasten their end. Accordingly the soldiers came and broke the legs of the two robbers, but when they came to Jesus they found that he was dead already. So they did not break any of his bones, but one of them pierced his side with a spear, and immediately blood and water flowed out.

In the evening, Joseph of Arimathea, a rich merchant who had secretly become a disciple of Jesus, went to Pilate and begged leave to take the body of Jesus and bury it. Pilate could hardly believe that he was so soon dead, so he called first for the officer in charge of the soldiers. When he had made sure from him that Jesus really was dead he gave leave for Joseph to take the body.

Joseph and Nicodemus, who had visited Jesus by night and become another of his secret followers, came and took the body away, wrapping it in clean linen with a mixture of herbs and spices.

On the west side of the hill where Jesus had been crucified there was a garden, in which was a new tomb that had never been used. This belonged to Joseph, who had it cut in the rock for himself, but now he was glad that he was able to take this last opportunity of giving it to his Lord. Quietly and carefully he and Nicodemus took the body of Jesus and buried it there.

Mary Magdalene and the wife of Cleopas, who had remained by the cross till the end, followed and sat close by, watching to see where they buried Jesus. They saw the men carry the body into the tomb, and then roll a great heavy stone across the entrance. After that they went home and prepared spices and perfumes to take to the grave. The next day, however, was the Sabbath, so they stayed at home until the first day of the following week.

On the day after the crucifixion, Caiaphas, with all the chief priests

They crucified him

and leaders of the Jews, went to Pontius Pilate. " Sir," they said to him, " we remember that when that man Jesus was alive he said that if he were killed he would come to life again within three days. Now we have come to ask you to give orders that the tomb shall be securely guarded until the third day, in case some of his disciples should come by night and steal the body, and then tell the people that he has come back to life. This second fraud would be even worse than the first."

But Pilate would not set a Roman guard. " You have your own guards," he replied. " Go and make the tomb as secure as you can."

That same evening, therefore, the chief priests stationed a guard of temple police outside the tomb. They also set a seal on the stone that stood across the entrance, so that they would know in the morning whether it had been moved. They had done everything possible to make sure that there was no fraud.

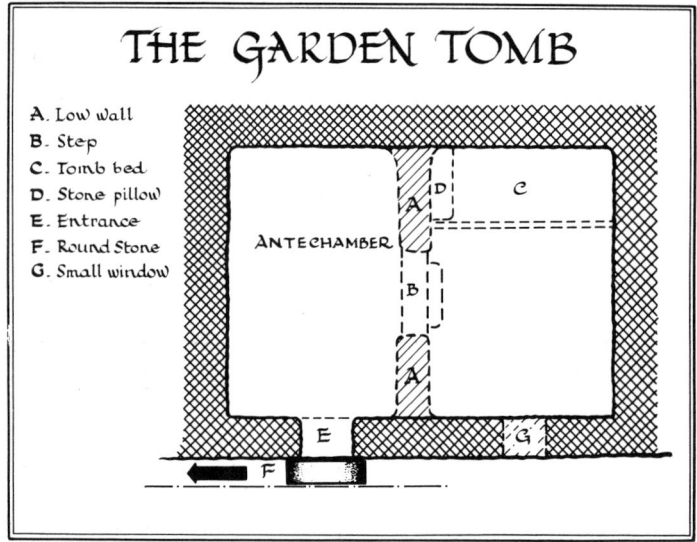

THE GARDEN TOMB

A. Low wall
B. Step
C. Tomb bed
D. Stone pillow
E. Entrance
F. Round Stone
G. Small window

ANTECHAMBER

The Empty Tomb

A T A very early hour in the morning, while the guards were dozing peacefully outside the tomb, they were suddenly startled by an earthquake. At the same time they saw an angel who came and rolled back the stone from the entrance and sat on it. The keepers were terrified and helpless when they saw him there, a glistening white figure shining in the darkness of the night; but after they had recovered from the first shock they fled as fast as they could into the city and told Caiaphas what had happened.

Mary Magdalene and the other women who had watched where Joseph had buried the body knew nothing about this. They had bought spices, and had agreed to take these to anoint the body in the morning. Very early, before it was light, they set out to the tomb.

The sun was just rising as Mary Magdalene and two of her companions entered the garden. They remembered what a heavy stone it was that Joseph had rolled across the entrance to the tomb, and they were saying to one another, " Who will roll away the stone for us from the door? "

When they came in sight of the tomb they were surprised to see that the stone had been rolled back. The narrow little entrance in the face of the rock was open and free for them to go in.

Mary hurried forward, but she had to stoop low to get in, because the doorway was barely three feet high. Once inside, she found herself in a small room with a low wall on her right. A gap in the middle of this led through to the burial chamber where the body was laid.

As Mary rose to her feet she noticed on her right a shaft of light which entered the burial chamber through a small window cut high up in the wall. Then suddenly she was terrified as she saw a figure dressed in a long white robe, sitting at the other side of the tomb.

It was a young man, and he began to speak: " Don't be afraid," he said; " I know that you are looking for Jesus who was crucified. But, look," he said, pointing to the back of the tomb where the shaft of light fell on the floor, " he is not here, for he has come to life again, as he told you. Come and see for yourself the place where he lay."

When Mary saw the white grave-clothes lying there on the stone she was more frightened than ever, and made for the doorway as fast as she could.

Meanwhile the young man went on, " Go and tell his disciples that he is risen from the dead and is going on to Galilee to meet them there.

" Remember what I have told you," he called, as Mary reached the open and ran as fast as she could to the city, followed by her two companions.

Mary Magdalene was a good deal younger than the other two women, and she soon left them far behind. She made straight for the house where John and Peter were staying, but by the time she got there she had quite forgotten what the young man in white had said.

" They have taken away the Lord out of the tomb," she gasped, " and we don't know where they have put him."

John and Peter, wondering who could have taken the body, set out at once for the tomb, both of them running. John ran faster than Peter, and got there first. Stooping down, he looked in through the entrance. Beyond the inner door he could see where the shaft of light from the window fell on the white grave-clothes. He could see that the body was not there.

Then Peter joined him and went right inside. He, too, saw the winding-sheet still lying in coils as if it had never been unwound from the body. The napkin which had covered the head still lay wound round by itself. Then John followed Peter into the tomb, and they both saw that although the body was gone the clothes had not been disturbed! It was not difficult to see what this meant—*no one* had taken the body: it had vanished on the spot! JESUS HAD RISEN FROM THE DEAD.

He is risen from the dead

RESURRECTION

Jesus Returns

WONDERING, and in silence, Peter and John returned to their lodgings in the city. There they heard a strange rumour. The guard which Caiaphas had stationed at the tomb the previous night had said that some of the followers of Jesus had come in the night and stolen the body while they slept. It was very strange that guards should admit that they were so neglectful that they had slept while they were on duty. Besides this, it was quite impossible for the disciples or anyone else to take the body without disturbing the grave-clothes.

Peter and John soon found out that when the terrified guards had come to report that an angel had rolled back the stone, the chief priests and rulers had held another meeting. After talking it over, they heavily bribed the guards to tell the story that the disciples had stolen the body.

Now after Mary Magdalene had seen Peter and John rush off to the tomb, she walked back in that direction herself, crying, and hardly knowing what she was doing. She could not understand how anyone could be so cruel as to take away the body of her Lord.

She was quite sure that none of the disciples could have done it. Peter and John were evidently quite as surprised as she was to learn that the body had gone; the others had all run away when Jesus was arrested, and probably had no idea where Jesus was buried.

Then she remembered that the chief priests had set a watch over the tomb specially to prevent the disciples taking the body. Had the guard, perhaps, stolen the body? No sooner had the idea entered her head than she saw how impossible it was: they were the very people who were there to prevent the body from disappearing.

At length she reached the tomb, and presently stooped down and looked in once more to make quite sure that the body was not there. Then she saw two angels dressed in white, sitting one at the head and the other at the feet of the place where the body of Jesus had been.

" Why are you crying? " one of them asked.

" Because they have taken away my Lord," she replied, " and I don't know where they have put him."

Turning back out of the tomb, she saw a man standing outside, but she did not know who it was.

" Why are you crying," he asked, " and whom are you looking for? "

Supposing him to be the gardener, she said, " Sir, if you have carried him away, please tell me where you have put him, and I will take him away."

" Mary! " he said; and immediately Mary knew that it was Jesus standing there.

" Master! " she cried, as she ran forward to fling her arms round him.

" Don't cling to me now," said Jesus, " but take this message to my friends: tell them to go to Galilee, and I will meet them there."

Then Jesus disappeared, and Mary ran to tell Peter and John that she had seen Jesus alive.

After Mary Magdalene had seen Jesus at the tomb her two companions also returned, together with certain other women, who were bringing spices. They, too, saw the angels in the tomb. At first they were frightened, but one of the angels said, " Why do you look for the living in the place of the dead? He is not here, but has come to life again. Remember how he told you in Galilee that he would be betrayed and crucified and then come to life again the third day."

At once they went to tell the other disciples, and suddenly, on the way, they saw Jesus coming to meet them.

" Don't be afraid," he said, " but go and tell my friends to go to Galilee, and I will meet them there."

The Mysterious Stranger

ON THAT same afternoon two of the disciples were walking to Emmaus, a village some seven or eight miles from Jerusalem. They were talking about the recent events when Jesus himself joined them. But he did not let them recognise him.

" What are you talking about? " he asked.

At this they stopped, looking sad; then one of them, named Cleopas, answered, " Are you a lonely stranger in Jerusalem, that you don't know what has been going on there these last few days? "

" What may that be? " Jesus asked.

" All about Jesus of Nazareth," they replied. " He was a prophet, mighty in word and deed before God and all the people. But the chief priests and rulers condemned him to death and crucified him. We were hoping that it would be he who would deliver Israel—and it was only the day before yesterday that all this happened.

" Then this morning some of the women of our company gave us a shock; they went to the tomb at dawn and found that his body was gone. They came and told us that they had seen a vision of angels, who had declared that he had come to life again. They even claimed that on the way to tell us about it they saw Jesus himself. Two of our party have, in fact, been to the tomb, and found everything just as the women had said, but they saw nothing of Jesus."

" You seem to be very dull," replied Jesus, " and very slow at believing all that the prophets have said. Did they not foretell that all these things would happen to the Christ before he set up his glorious kingdom? "

" We have always believed that the Christ would be a great king," they answered, " and it was only a week ago that Jesus came riding into Jerusalem on the foal of an ass. We thought then that the old prophecy was fulfilled which said, ' Rejoice, O Jerusalem: see, your king is coming to you. He is just but humble, riding upon an ass, even the foal of an ass '."

" You were quite right," said Jesus, " but first he must suffer and

122

be crucified. Have you not noticed how exactly a crucifixion is described in that psalm which begins, ' My God, my God, why hast thou forsaken me? ' "

" Why, of course! " cried Cleopas. " Jesus started to recite that psalm just as he was dying. Those were his very words. He must have said that to remind us of the psalm."

" Yes, " said his friend, " we ought not to have forgotten the verse which says, ' They pierced my hands and my feet.' And then there is that other one which tells of the sweat caused by the awful pain, and the bones of the hands and shoulders being out of joint: ' I am poured out like water, and all my bones are out of joint '."

" I remember some more verses now," added Cleopas. " ' All they that see me laugh me to scorn. They shake their heads and sneer, saying, He trusted in God that he would deliver him; let him deliver him now.' That is exactly what the people were shouting when Jesus was on the cross."

" Yes," went on his friend, " and I can tell you another verse out of that same psalm which came true. ' They part my garments among them and draw lots for my coat.' That is what the soldiers did with his clothes."

As they walked on their way to Emmaus, Jesus went on to show them how many of the events of the past week had been foretold long years before by Moses and the prophets: When at last they came to the end of their journey it was getting towards evening, so they asked Jesus to come in and stay the night with them; but they still did not know that it was Jesus.

When they sat down to supper Jesus took bread, broke it and gave it to them in the way he had taught the disciples at their last supper before he was betrayed. Then it was that they recognised who he was, but immediately Jesus disappeared.

" We ought to have known who it was," they said one to another, " by the way he explained all those Scriptures to us."

They were so excited about their talk with Jesus that they set off back to Jerusalem at once to tell their friends. But in Jerusalem the rumour had got round which the guards at the tomb had been paid to spread. People were saying that the disciples of Jesus had stolen his body in order to convince everyone that Jesus had risen from the dead.

Cleopas and his friend arrived back late that night, and found that the other disciples were having a meeting behind locked doors because they were afraid of the Jews. They were discussing what could have happened to the body of Jesus. Peter and John said they were quite sure that Jesus had come to life again, just as the women had said; in fact, Peter told them that he himself had seen Jesus that same afternoon. Others of them were doubtful, and told Peter that he and the women must have imagined it, or else seen a ghost.

" But who could have taken the body? " one of them kept on asking. There was no answer to this at all. It would have needed at least two or three strong men to move the stone and to carry the corpse. The Romans had no reason whatever to take the body away. The chief priests and Jews certainly did not take it, for they had even set a guard to see that it remained in the tomb. And none of the followers of Jesus would have taken it, because they were all honest men. The greatest mystery was the fact that the grave-clothes were left behind, and were still lying in coils, as if they had never been unwound from the body.

The disciples had much to talk and argue about that night.

Why Jesus Died

IT WAS while the disciples were discussing the disappearance of the body of Jesus that Cleopas and his friend came back from Emmaus and told them how they had talked with Jesus on the road that very afternoon. They began to explain what Jesus had said about the old prophecies which had foretold how Christ must first suffer on the cross before he could set up his kingdom. This led to further problems.

" Why should the Christ first have to die? " one of them asked. " Why could he not set up his kingdom right away? "

They were still puzzling over this when Jesus himself appeared. " Peace be with you," he said.

They were all startled and frightened, for they thought they were seeing a ghost, and could not understand how he had got in, because all the doors were locked.

" Why such a panic? " asked Jesus. " I am no ghost. See my hands and my feet; it is my real self. Feel me and see: a ghost has no flesh and bones as you see that I have." And he showed them his hands and his feet where the nails had been.

While they could still hardly believe it was true for sheer wonder and joy, he asked them, " Have you anything to eat? "

They gave him some grilled fish, and after he had eaten it they asked him why the Christ must first be crucified before he could set up his kingdom.

" Have you not read in the Scriptures," Jesus explained, " that the heart of man is deceitful above all things, and desperately wicked; and you know the wicked cannot enter my kingdom. David also says, ' When the Lord looked down from heaven on the children of men, to see if there were any that would understand and seek God, he saw that all had gone astray, and all become wicked: there was none righteous; no, not one.' But the Scriptures also say, ' the soul that sinneth, it shall die,' so it follows that all men are doomed to death."

127

As Jesus quoted these words each man knew that in the eyes of God he was a sinner and deserved to die, for indeed there was none righteous; no, not one.

"But," Jesus continued, "God has declared from the beginning that if a sinner repents, he will accept the death of one who has done no wrong in his place. Adam was told that in the day that he ate the forbidden fruit he should surely die, but when God clothed him with the skins of animals he showed that by their death his sin was covered. So Moses also taught you to sacrifice goats and bulls as a sin-offering each year.

"All these sacrifices," said Jesus, "were only signs of what was to come, for the blood of bulls and goats cannot themselves take away sins. They were signs to show that the Christ would come to offer himself as the only perfect sacrifice of one who had done no wrong, and suffer the penalty for the sins of the world.

"As Isaiah has said, 'Surely it was our pains which he bore, it was our sorrows he carried; yet we thought he was struck down and smitten by God. But it was for our sins that he was wounded and for our wrongs that he was bruised; it was for our good that he was whipped, and with his stripes we are healed. For, surely, like sheep we have all gone astray, and have followed our own desires; but the Lord has laid upon him the guilt of us all'."

The disciples had no doubt that Jesus had done no wrong; Pilate himself had said so time after time. When they remembered this, and how Jesus had been whipped and tormented and finally crucified, they saw that in all these sufferings he had been bearing their punishment for them.

As Jesus went on reminding them of this old prophecy they saw how Isaiah had foretold the events of his trial and death: "'He was treated unfairly yet he did not complain: he was brought as a lamb to be slaughtered, and as a sheep in the hands of the shearers is dumb, so he did not open his mouth.

"'He was condemned unjustly, and no one cared what became of him: he was cut off from the land of the living and struck down for the wrongs of his people. He came to his death among criminals, and made his grave with the rich; though he himself had done no violence, nor spoken a wrong word '."

How remarkably true all this was! For Jesus had been crucified between two robbers and then buried in a rich man's grave. Yet Isaiah had written it more than seven hundred years before it happened.

When Jesus had explained these Scriptures to them he added, " Thus it is written that the Christ would suffer and then come back to life again on the third day. And this shall be told to all men and all nations, so that whoever may be truly sorry for the wrong he has done, and believes that I am the Christ and that I have suffered and died for him, shall be forgiven. Then I will cleanse him from all evil and will put a new spirit within him, to cause him to obey all my laws willingly, and he shall have everlasting life. You are the witnesses of these things: as my Father has sent me, even so I send you." And with that he left them.

Now Thomas was not among the disciples when Jesus had come to them, so they told him later that Jesus had shown himself to them, but he would not believe them.

" Unless I shall see in his hands the marks of the nails," he said, " and put my finger into the wounds and my hand into his side, I will not believe it."

A week later the disciples again met together, and this time Thomas was with them when Jesus appeared.

" Peace be with you," he said, and then, turning to Thomas, he went on, " Come over here and look at my hands; and stretch out your hand and put it into my side. Do not be faithless any more, but believe."

" You are my Lord and my God," exclaimed Thomas, as he knelt at the feet of Jesus and worshipped him.

" Thomas," said Jesus, " you have believed because you have seen me; blessed are those who believe although they have not seen me."

His Last Instructions

OON after Thomas and the other disciples had seen Jesus they all went home to Galilee as he had told them. One night Peter and some of the others went out fishing on the lake. In the morning they were coming in to land when they saw Jesus on the shore, but they did not know who it was.

" Have you got any fish? " he called to them.

" No! " they replied.

" Well, cast your net on the right side of the ship," he said.

When they had done this they caught such a large number of fish that they could hardly pull the net in.

" It must be Jesus," said John, remembering a previous wonderful catch.

So they all scrambled ashore as fast as they could, while Jesus lighted a fire and cooked them a breakfast of bread and fish.

When they had eaten the meal with him, Jesus turned to Peter and said, " Simon Peter, do you love me? "

" Yes, Lord," Peter replied. " You know I love you."

" Then feed my sheep," answered Jesus.

Then, because Peter had denied him three times, Jesus asked him a second and a third time, " Peter, do you love me? "

Three times Peter was able to say, " Yes, Lord, you know I love you." And Jesus showed that he had not only forgiven Peter, but trusted him completely, by asking him to look after his flock.

For nearly six weeks after his resurrection Jesus showed himself in this way to his friends, and gave them many clear proofs that he was really alive. On one occasion he was seen by five hundred of them at once. During this time he taught them about the kingdom of God, saying that one day he would return to earth in power and great glory to reign as King of Israel over the whole world.

" You have read in the Scriptures," he said, " that the Lord will a second time gather his people from all the lands where they have been driven, even from the isles of the sea. For the day will come,

He was carried up into the sky

when people will no longer speak of the Lord God who brought up the children of Israel out of Egypt, but of the Lord God who brought up and led the house of Israel out of the north country, and from all the countries where they have been scattered.

" Then they shall see the Son of Man coming in the clouds of heaven, and he shall be given dominion and glory and an everlasting kingdom, in which all people, nations and languages shall serve him. At that time the dead who have put their trust in him shall rise from their graves with immortal bodies, and those who are alive at that time will be changed and be like them, and they shall live with the Lord for ever."

One day, as the disciples were sitting on the Mount of Olives and Jesus was telling them about these things, they asked him when it would be time for him to set up this kingdom which the prophets had foretold.

" It is not for you to know the exact time," he told them, " for as in the days of Noah before the flood, people were eating and drinking and caring nothing for God, until suddenly the flood came and took them all away, so shall it be when the Son of Man comes; but all will not be left in darkness, that that day should come on them unexpectedly. For you are my witnesses, to preach this message both in Judaea and in Samaria and to the ends of the earth."

When he had said this he was carried up into the sky and they saw him no more. But while they still stood gazing upwards two men clothed in white suddenly appeared and said, " Why do you stand there looking up into the sky? This very same Jesus who has been taken up from you into heaven will come again in just the same way as you have seen him go."

From that time, and beginning from Jerusalem, the disciples taught that Jesus had come to life again and had been carried up to heaven, and that all who believe in him shall be saved and have everlasting life.

Bible References

THE KING IS BORN
The Good News   Luke 1. 26-35; Mat. 1. 18-23; Luke 2. 1-20. Also Isaiah 7. 14
Escape from Murder .   .   .   .   .   Mat. 2. 1-23. Also Micah 5. 2
Lost in Jerusalem . . . . Luke 2. 41-52

HIS TASK BEGINS
Preparing the Way Mat. 3. 1-17; Mark 1. 2-11; Luke 3. 1-22. Also Malachi 3. 1;
Isaiah 40. 3; Daniel 9. 25
Wrong Ways Mat. 4. 1-11; Mark 1. 12-13; Luke 4. 1-13. Also Deut. 8. 3; 6. 13;
6. 16; Psalm 91. 11-12
Choosing his Men . . . . . John 1. 29-51. Also Isaiah 40. 3

VISITS TO THE CAPITAL
Driving out the Robbers .   .   .   .   .   . John 2. 13-3. 22
The Woman at the Well .   .   .   .   .   . John 4. 1-43
In Trouble for Doing Good . . . . John 5. 1-47

TEACHING IN GALILEE
Promises Come True . . . . . Luke 4. 16-30. Also Isaiah 61. 1-2
Friends at Home .   .   . Mat. 4. 13-24; 8. 14-17; Mark 1. 16-34; Luke 4. 31-41
Catching Fish .   .   .   .   .   . Mark 4. 35-39; Luke 4. 42-5. 11

THE PHARISEES MAKE TROUBLE
The Trouble Starts .   Mat. 8. 2-4; 9. 2-8; Mark 1. 40-2. 12; Luke 5. 12-26
The Tax Collector .   .   Mat. 9. 9-13; Mark 2. 13-17; Luke 5. 27-32
Fault-finding   Mat. 9. 14-17; 12. 1-14; Mark 2. 18-3. 6; Luke 5. 33-6. 11.
Also Hosea 6. 6

THE KINGDOM EXPLAINED
Lessons on the Hillside Mat. 12. 15-21; 4. 25-7. 29; Mark 3. 7-19; Luke 6. 12-49.
Also Isaiah 42. 1-3
Help for a Roman .   .   .   .   .   . Mat. 8. 5-13; Luke 7. 1-10
Help for a Jew .   .   .   .   . Mark 4. 1-5, 43; Luke 7. 11-8. 56

HEAVENLY FOOD
Feeding the Five Thousand Mat. 14. 1-21; Mark 6. 7-44; Luke 9. 1-17; John 6. 1-14
The Bread of Life .   .   . Mat. 14. 22-23; Mark 6. 45-52; John 6. 15-71

JESUS WITH HIS MEN
Avoiding Danger . .   .   .   . Mat. 15. 1-16. 12; Mark 7. 1-8. 21
Plan for Victory . . . Mat. 16. 13-17. 9; Mark 8. 27-9. 10; Luke 9. 18-36
Power for Victory . . . Mat. 17. 14-21; Mark 9. 14-32; Luke 9. 37-43

BACK IN JERUSALEM

JEALOUS JEWS

THE FINAL CONTEST

THE TRIAL

THE LAST SACRIFICE

RESURRECTION

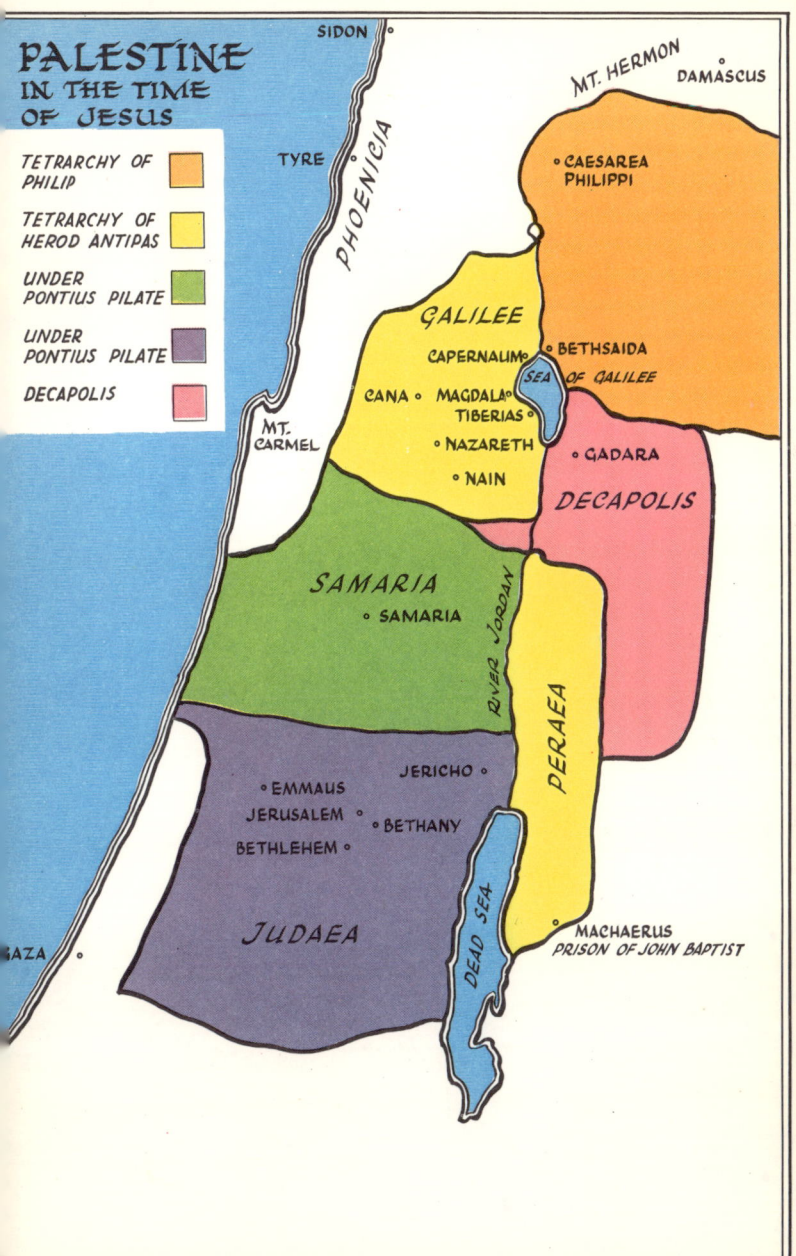

PALESTINE
IN THE TIME OF JESUS

- TETRARCHY OF PHILIP
- TETRARCHY OF HEROD ANTIPAS
- UNDER PONTIUS PILATE
- UNDER PONTIUS PILATE
- DECAPOLIS

SIDON

MT. HERMON

DAMASCUS

TYRE

PHOENICIA

° CAESAREA PHILIPPI

GALILEE

CAPERNAUM °

° BETHSAIDA

SEA OF GALILEE

CANA °

° MAGDALA

TIBERIAS °

° NAZARETH

° GADARA

° NAIN

DECAPOLIS

MT. CARMEL

SAMARIA

° SAMARIA

RIVER JORDAN

PERAEA

JERICHO °

° EMMAUS

JERUSALEM °

° BETHANY

BETHLEHEM °

DEAD SEA

JUDAEA

GAZA °

° MACHAERUS
PRISON OF JOHN BAPTIST